I Never Had A Proper Job

First published in 2012 by
Liberties Press
7 Rathfarnham Road | Terenure | Dublin 6W
Tel: +353 (1) 405 5701
www.libertiespress.com | info@libertiespress.com

Trade enquiries to Gill & Macmillan Distribution
Hume Avenue | Park West | Dublin 12
T: +353 (1) 500 9534 | F: +353 (1) 500 9595 | E: sales@gillmacmillan.ie

Distributed in the UK by
Turnaround Publisher Services
Unit 3 | Olympia Trading Estate | Coburg Road | London N22 6TZ
T: +44 (0) 20 8829 3000 | E: orders@turnaround-uk.com

Distributed in the United States by
Dufour Editions | PO Box 7 | Chester Springs | Pennsylvania 19425

ISBN: 978-1-907593-40-6
2 4 6 8 10 9 7 5 3 1

A CIP record for this title is available from the British Library.

Cover design by Sin É Design
Internal design by Liberties Press
Printed by Nørhaven

The publishers gratefully acknowledge
financial assistance from the Arts Council.

I Never Had A Proper Job

A Life in the Theatre

Barry Cassin

For Nancy

1

North of Nenagh, on the road to Dublin, stands a railway bridge. Forty years ago, driving home after the opening of a John B. Keane play in the Cork Opera House, I reached the bridge and did what I had promised to do for many a day: I turned left onto the road to Cloughjordan. I drove slowly, searching, scanning right and left.

Suddenly, there it was, back from the road, smaller than I had recalled, as places are when reality is superimposed on childhood memory. Not bad, I told myself, to recognise the house where I was born at eight o'clock on a Sunday morning in the year of grace 1924, and which, according to family lore, I left before I could walk when the family moved to Nenagh. I stopped and gazed. It felt good to have found my starting point.

Before I set off on this casual memoir of my years in the theatre, I must record that many years later I passed that way again, this time to play in a film shot in Patrick Bergin's castle near Cloughjordan. Like looking forward to greeting an old friend, I prepared once more to meet my birthplace. But I found no trace of it. I drove on and back, and on again. The house was gone. A pebble of my life had been swept away.

Long-ago days are yellowing snapshots. Attached to the crossbar of my father's bicycle is a child's saddle with a backrest and stirrups. So high am I perched that I can see over the hedge into O'Brien's field. 'That's where you were found,' my father tells me, 'under a cabbage leaf.' So much for the facts of life.

From the floor I look up at my mother dipping floury hands into a mixing bowl on the kitchen table. Sunlight streaming in from a window at her back casts a halo of light about her. She looks down at me and smiles. I feel secure.

A dog comes to mind. He guards his master's doorway. His owner plays boxing with me. I strike at him. The dog is on me, leaving teeth marks on my stomach. Everyone makes excuses for the dog.

Many years on, visiting Nenagh to direct a play for the local drama group, I put my memory into overdrive and sought the house where I was bitten, and found it with unexpected ease. It was as I remembered, sunlight angling in, a geranium on a windowsill, a wagtail fluttering. I was tempted to knock on the door and ask to see inside. But why? I was thirty years of age and the past had yet no sentimental significance for me.

But a memory had been stirred of peering up and down the street in fear of the bully who might accost me on the way to school. We shared a desk. He prodded me and pinched, and I suffered his torturing until the day he went too far, the day he spat on me. I blew my top, let loose and belted him, right on the conk. A bit of luck. I hadn't

aimed, just lashed out. He bled; I walked home with my head held
high. I was seven years old.

My father was born in Ballyneal, near New Ross where three counties
meet: Kilkenny, Wexford and Waterford. Of his large family I knew
only Statia, who lived on the farm, the home place, and much later
Philip, when he visited from America. The family were all born well
before the end of the 1800s, and the emigrant ship dispersed them to
America and England. Emigration was taken for granted as part of
Irish life. Young Irish people, working in England, crowded ships and
trains on the way home at Christmas, those in America sent cards and
money or simply disappeared, whether through indifference or failed
fortunes, or worse, none would ever learn.

In the seventies, while adjudicating at a drama festival in New
Ross, I resolved to seek out the farm. At the bridge of Ballyneal,
memories flooded back. I followed the road uphill as far as a lane on
the left, then down the lane past houses scattered on either side, until
I reached a farmyard. There was the house, the half-door, the well, the
haggard. Had the wheel-bellows survived? In the evening firelight I
had turned it when neighbours gathered to welcome my father and
chat about this one living with the married sister since the farming
got too much for him, and that one dead this couple of years, God
rest him.

In the evening the talk turned to the country and the crops, the old
days, and the mighty men of yore. And hurling. Always hurling. My
father grew up with the GAA. Like many young men of his time the
national games gave him a pride in place, an identity and added
stature when Kilkenny won a championship. Great players of the past

forever strode the pitches of his imagination – Sim Walton, 'Drug' Walsh, Matt Gargan, The Graces – no more than names to me, but listening to him I almost believed I'd seen them play; and once trapped by the legends and the lore there was no question of my allegiance. Kilkenny was my team, then and forever.

In 1931, my father was transferred from Nenagh to Monaghan. Nat Ross, Removals transported our furniture, while the family travelled by train and stayed overnight in Dublin. Mother engaged a horse cab to carry us to the Ormond Hotel, where we would spend the night. On the journey from the station, she explained that Dublin people were small because city air was not as fresh as country air. Barefoot children were 'the poor', beggars were 'the poor', as was the woman with the club foot, who dragged a bucket to and from a wayside pump, and the pallid children of Nenagh who must be avoided because they might have head lice or be reeking of TB.

Next day, when Mother was shopping in O'Connell Street, a veiled woman, all in black, swept past. 'Maud Gonne MacBride,' she said in awe, 'in widow's weeds until Ireland is set free.'

'Herself and Robert Emmet,' my father scoffed.

On the train north, when we traversed the viaduct at Drogheda, I was held at the window so that I might look down on a mighty river. 'The Boyne,' I was told, 'that King Billy crossed when a cowardly English king ran away and let the Irish down.' Who was King Billy? Who was the cowardly English king? No one explained but I was warned that we were entering the 'Black North'.

'Why is it black?'

'Black Protestants.'

'Are they black like the black babies I put pennies in a box for the African Missions to convert?'

'Don't be silly,' said a sister.

'They're waiting for you in Monaghan with cleavers and toma-hawks,' said another.

'Nonsense,' said my mother. 'Protestants are just like us.'

'They don't go to mass,' I said.

'They go to church.'

'If they're just like us, why don't they go to mass?'

'That's enough about it. Read your comic.'

A constant complaint of my father was that the Post Office provided no dwelling house for its postmasters. 'Banks look after their managers but not my crowd. We must fend for ourselves.' Which was not easy in the 1930s, a time of economic stress. Vacant houses were few, new houses fewer. When my father was transferred, he was forced to grab whatever was available in any town to which he was posted. In Monaghan what was available was Cappagh Lodge, once the home of long-departed country gentry. Huge beyond our needs, it lay amongst trees three miles outside the town, long, low and white. 'A terrible barracks of a place,' Mother wailed.

A curving, tree-lined avenue led to a gravelled cartilage. The entrance hall, as large as a living-room, was dominated by a marble fireplace at which my father stood, hands clasped behind him, and dreamed of a time of squires and stirrup-cups. Upstairs were echoing bedrooms powdered with fallen plaster and looped with cobwebs. Off the downstairs hall, rooms opened one from the other like Russian dolls. 'My God,' my father mused, 'it must have cost a fortune to keep up a place like this. Gone now, the family who built it. Or broke. At least they weren't burnt out by our national patriots.'

Houses such as Cappagh, many in disrepair, dotted the Irish countryside, evidence of the decline of the landlord class, at sea in the young republic, in due course to be ripe subjects for the drama and literature of a new generation. One thinks of Elizabeth Bowen's mansion in Bowen's Court and Lennox Robinson's *Killycreggs in Twilight*. Some of the Big Houses survived, if not the families who had occupied them, and, in an ironic turnabout, give employment still, the butler and the parlour maid replaced by the hotel manager and the tour guide.

We lived in one wing of Cappagh. On winter mornings, breath clouded over a weight of blankets. Taps froze, pipes juddered. On bath night, kettles of boiling water had to be carried from the basement kitchen, far below. My father had first use of the hot water, myself the last. Towels steamed on the clothes-horse at the kitchen range. Mother's vigorous towelling was a little treasury of love.

Rats were established residents in Cappagh long before we arrived. They were everywhere; in the kitchen, on the stairs, in the sitting room, scampering in the gutter pipe, scuffling in the back yard. My father laid poison right and left. 'Bastards!' he yelled.

The back lane opened on to the Scotstown Road near Connolly's Bridge. On a fine evening my father and I dropped pebbles on a resting trout and laughed when it twitched and darted upstream. Under the bridge flashed a kingfisher, keeping pace with his mirrored image in the water. 'Look at him!' my father cried. 'Look at him, boy. The colours of him.'

Connolly's Bridge was a halt for Henry Cassidy's bus before it rattled on to Ballinode and the border area of Scotstown. As a special treat it was arranged that I would do the full round perched beside the driver, who would look after me.

A man with a stubbled face leaned over me, 'Where are you from, son?'

I was a townie, unaccustomed to interrogation from a countryman with cow dung on his boots. My voice faltered. I whispered, 'Nenagh.'

'What's that you said?'

'Nenagh.'

'I can't hear you. Is there something wrong with you?'

The bus driver came to my rescue. 'Nenagh. His father is the new postmaster in Monaghan town.'

'Nenagh? Where's that?'

'In the south someplace.'

'It's a wonder they'd send a man and his family all that way. Could they not find someone from around here?'

'That's the way of the Post Office crowd.'

'They're a quare crowd so.'

The man stared out at rushy fields and undernourished stock. He spat on the floor of the bus and crushed the splatter with his boot. 'We're giving away the calves for nothing. And the priest scrugin' up his face when he reads the Dues. It's well for him with a big house and no family. A bob I give at Christmas and Easter. I'd give more but how can I with the childer living on castor oil?'

The bus chugged on. Men raised their heads to watch it pass, its comings and goings dividing the slogging sameness of their days. Rounding a corner, it slowed to give passage to a wheeled trolley that bore a legless man who pushed himself along with sticks he used like oars. He was a latter-day Johnny I Hardly Knew You with his begging bowl, human detritus of the Great War, one of many to be encountered when I was young, the flotsam and jetsam of Vimy Ridge, Ypres, the Somme or Passchendaele. Some rode in pram-wheeled boxes, begging as they went, others had plates where their skulls had been laid open by shrapnel, some were shell-shocked and mute, one forever bayoneted Germans and bellowed when he went over an imaginary top. My father gave generously to these maimed men. Like them, he had fought for the Allies in France. He had returned unharmed but they had paid the soldier's price.

My father's district included a number of sub-post offices that had to be regularly 'checked'. When he was on his rounds, he liked Mother or myself to accompany him, and, if relations between him and the sub-postmaster or sub-postmistress were good, if he was not wearing his thunderous scowl, Mother and I were invited in for tea in the kitchen. Open hearth, steaming kettle, crooning hens peering in the open door. Or, if things were on a grander scale, tea and seed cake in the parlour.

In country homes the parlour was little used. It was stiff with formality and dim behind lace curtains, reserved for the visits of the Parish Priest, the doctor, relations home from the States, the clean-shod and individuals of local consequence. Parlours were half-worlds lodged between the present and the past, gravely silent, that silence amplified by the muted sounds of beast or cart from the outside world. Parlours were museums of stuffed birds under glass bell-jars and the sepia portrait of a bridal couple stiff with wedding-day embarrassment. On the walls hung a picture of the Pope, a Home-Sweet-Home, a Sacred Heart and a Papal Blessing. Great Aunt Sarah, in her oval of silver, rubbed shoulders on the sideboard with the trophy won by Uncle Tommy on a sports day long ago. Parlours were little repositories of a life, long gone, and fond memories preserved.

In one of those parlours my father never failed to call for the Dancing Man. 'For the young lad,' he would say, 'who might never see another.' (And indeed I did not until a lifetime later when Liam Clancy produced a similar novelty to entertain his audience.)

The Dancing Man was a marionette with jointed limbs, a wooden farmer dressed in his Sunday best of black suit and polished boots. Fixed to his back was a rod by which the sub-postmistress, a merry lady all in black, held him upright, his feet touching a miniature platform. Lilting, she tapped out a dancing measure on the platform that brought to life the Dancing Man's feet, stepping, cutting, rattling out the rhythm like a kettle drum.

That rhythm I recalled, years afterwards, when a vigorous old man danced on the flagstones of a country pub. I was as old, then, as was my father when I sat with him in that long-ago parlour, old enough to understand that he had not requested the Dancing Man for my sake but for his own. The Dancing Man was his past remembered as, in turn, the beat of the old man's dancing feet was my own past revisited, the rhythm marking a time when I was a child and all was wondrous and new.

My earliest memory of theatre is of a small girl dressed in rags and wearing a wide-brimmed hat. On her arm she carries a basket of flowers. One hand proffers a posy of violets while she sings:

> *There are many sad and weary*
> *In this dreary world of ours,*
> *Crying in the night so bitter*
> *Won't you buy my pretty flowers?*

I was in the village hall in Ballinode. My mother and I had walked half a mile from Cappagh Lodge to a local concert. It was winter, frost in the air, oil lamps yellow, stars overhead. Who else performed in the concert I have long since forgotten. I remember only the little girl singing her sentimental Victorian ballad. When she floats into memory I am reminded of a small boy enraptured by a costume and a song, a boy enthralled by a world of make-believe.

In my home, any mention of 'the War' meant the Great War, my father's war. A Redmondite, he was over thirty when he volunteered and spent four years in France from 1915. His rank was Lance Corporal. He claimed that he had lived through it because he was in communications and operated behind the front lines. Each evening he marched his men back to the billet, at the crossroads giving the order 'Right turn'. One evening, not knowing why, he ordered 'Left turn', and his company had proceeded no more than a hundred yards when a shell fell where they would have been had they turned right. What had made him change the order? 'The Rosary,' he told me, 'I never missed a night.'

Often, in those pre-television times, before an evening's entertainment was to goggle at the box, my father would summon me and we would set off together. He carried a walking stick for fashion, not from need. He walked briskly, his shoulders back, and I lengthened my step to keep pace with his army stride. On a frosty night, when footsteps rang from the iron tips of our walking shoes, and potholes were a sheen of ice, his stick arched over us, pointing out the Milky Way. He spoke of the unfathomable distance to the nearest star, of the overwhelming vastness of the galaxy, and of how space went on and on into infinity.

That memory is a vivid snapshot in my album of the past: two figures on a frosty road, a man, his son, and a walking stick sweeping across a gleaming sky. When I try to come to terms with eternity, I draw on that image, my father and myself gazing into the nobility of space with no television presenter to trivialise our astonishment with facts and graphics.

We knew a marvel when we saw one.

It was my mother's continued hope of finding 'somewhere liveable', and not 'a barracks of a place', three-and-a-half miles outside the town, permanently at war with the damp, the isolation and the rats, that drove us from house to house. After a couple of years in Cappagh Lodge we moved to Corlatt House, a mile beyond Monaghan cathedral on the Dublin road. Though not as vast as Cappagh, it was large enough to be converted, in later years, into a boys' school.

I grew to love old houses, with their tantalising ambience of the past: the faded square of wallpaper where a picture once hung, the slack bell-pull that rang no bell, the broken window rope and a shutter hanging loose. In Corlatt House I spent much time alone. Off the upstairs passageway was my playroom. It contained no furniture, and a candle was my only light. There I played my solitary games and lost myself in the thousand-and-one stories of Scheherazade.

Candlelight adds texture and mystery to surroundings. In my playroom nothing moved but the waver of the candle flame. The picture framed by the uncurtained window altered with the fading of evening from a silhouette of branches outside to a black translucent image of the room where I was sitting. In that reflection I saw myself, the image of a boy studying the image of himself, fascinated by his own transparency. With the candle held aloft I was insubstantial like a ghost, my playroom transported outside the window, and in that reflected world I dragged at the edges of dream and reality until they fused, happy to lose myself in a double world. I peopled it with companions, one true beyond all others. He was my comrade when I listened on one elbow to the voices of my parents conversing in low, bedtime voices in the adjoining bedroom. If times were good, I heard the gossip of the day, the trivialities that make up the desultory rhythm of pillow talk. Sometimes the explosion came from nothing; more often the signs were in the air for days, my father's unease and my mother's defensive, deepening silences. The good times did not last and lava fell on all of us.

When the eruption came, there was turmoil downstairs, my father raging, my mother speaking low or not at all, then her step on the stairs, and me pretending to be asleep when she looked into my room. I could hear my father prowl from room to room as if in search of something he could not find, I would hear the hall door slam and his steps crunch on the gravel until his furious march was ended and he came upstairs to bed. Then silence, but no one in the house was sleeping. Next day the silence would persist, and for many days, until remorse and weariness brought a sort of truce. Nothing would change, but in the good times I could pretend.

For a time we lived in Tranquilla, a solid, quadrate house half-a-mile outside the town on the Clones Road, a short cycle for my father to the Post Office, a brief walk for my three sisters to the St Louis Convent and an easy walk for shopping or to Sunday mass.

Our old enemies, the rats, thundered in the attic. They dug archways through the skirting boards. A whooping sister with a poker chased a rat from under a sitting room armchair and, once, when my mother stooped to pick up a bucket in the yard a rat ran up her arm and down her back. In old houses the battle against the rats was never won.

It was in Tranquilla that my father had – what shall I call it? – an experience. A high wind was blowing when he set off up the stairs to plug a window that was rattling – rattling windows, barking dogs, twittering swallows in the gutter pipe always put him 'on edge'. Halfway up the stairs we heard him stop, then quickly come down again.

'What's wrong?'

'Nothing.' But his candle was trembling.

It was some time before I learned what had happened. When he was going up the stairs, he felt someone, something, a presence, descending from above. He neither saw nor heard anything, but *it*, whatever *it* was, brushed past him, backing him against the wall.

From then on, for as long as we lived in that house, thoughts of *something* on the stairs sent shivers down my spine. It frightened me much more than did 'The Knock', which my father heard at night – Rap . . . rap-rap. Rap . . . rap-rap – like knuckles on a wooden door, a warning of death in his family. The next morning he would announce, 'Another one gone,' and too often he was right.

I considered The Knock a talent special to my father, like water divining or bone-setting. When I was older I began to doubt his gift. It was no more than imagination, I decided, a flair for the theatrical heightened by news of a relative who was seriously ill. I did my father wrong. Many years ahead, when his favourite brother, Philip, died in America, and he was aware of it before the news arrived, I would have all the proof I needed that my father had a unique awareness of death when it touched his family.

On summer holidays in Bettystown, County Meath, in a local hall now disappeared with its memories of raffles, Housey-Housey, jumble sales and summer hops, I received a blooding in a kind of theatre far different from Anew McMaster's Shakespearean offerings – melodrama, with its twirling moustaches, noble heroes, sneering villains, and heroines above reproach. Even the ill-fated Maria Marten, heroine of the tragedy that bears her name, still retained an ineffable aura of virginity after her seduction by the villainous William Corder, thanks to a moralistic Victorian sleight of hand.

A scratch company presented a summer season and my mother, always a good one for a show, brought me along. It was my first time to see such stock-in-trade barnstormers as *The Face at the Window*, *The Limping Man* and the most famous tear-jerker of them all, *East Lynne*, with an offspring of the company or, indeed, a slim adult actress press-ganged into service, decked in a baby bonnet and curled up in the cradle as Little Willie. Later in life I would play in *East Lynne* and recall the deathless utterance of Lady Isobel over the prostrate body of her child, 'Dead, dead, and never called me Mother,' a line delivered with relish by any actress worth her salt, even though it is nowhere to be found in the novel by Mrs Henry Wood.

I idolised the actors. I ingratiated myself into their afternoon cricket matches on the beach, and the nightly blood-curdler lost none of its tingle by knowing that, earlier that afternoon, the face behind the waxed moustache had lost his wicket to one of my demon deliveries. When the curtain rose, the make-believe had me in thrall.

My first time on stage was in the annual school opera, *Rob o' the Forest* – an operetta to be accurate, but 'opera' we called it and opera it remained – a tale of jolly bandits who robbed the rich to feed the poor and led the sheriff a merry dance –

> *Rob o' the forest, helm and pike a flash,*
> *Rob o' the forest, sword and dagger a clash*
> *King of the woodland, scourge of the countryside*
> *Bravest and boldest, laws and sheriffs defied.*

I didn't want to have anything to do with *Rob o' the Forest*, but there was as much chance of dodging the school opera as there was of dodging Sunday mass.

I was still awkward in the presence of girls and did not know where to look when a bevy of fiddlers and cellists trooped in from the convent to play in the orchestra. Rehearsal was bad enough with a coven of giggling females gazing up sardonically from the pit, but it was nothing to what lay ahead at the dress rehearsal.

There is no agony to match the torture of being the butt of school-girl sniggering, which is what greeted the entrance of our greenwood chorus, a bumbling line of gawky boys attired in ill-fitting green costumes and pointy hats, looking like an invasion of overgrown garden gnomes. It was not the slashed jerkins, slaved over by our mothers, that was the problem, but the baggy knee-breeches that shamelessly outlined my manhood with all the style of a pair of convent passion-killers. In the orchestra pit the harpies giggled.

If I did not get much of a kick out of being a greenwood bandit, I got a huge kick out of being a king the following year. When I was informed that I was under consideration for a part, I assumed that, not being a singer, it was for a speaking, not a singing, part. But no, there was a solo – I hadn't a hope. The music teacher stood me at the piano, I croaked a bar or two and she closed the piano. That was that. I was dished.

But triumph was to be mine. The solo was dropped, and for three performances I lorded it in cotton wool ermine and a cardboard crown. Backstage, in my hearing, a lady said, 'The boy is very good,' and no film star paraded up the red carpet to receive an Oscar with an ego bigger than mine as I swanned around the town for days.

Then, without warning, there was competition. Her name was Siobhán, an unusual name in an era of Marys, Kathleens, Noras and Bernadettes. With my mother I went along to see her perform in *The Geisha* in the local convent, and the longer I watched, the greener grew my jealousy, because this Siobhán McKenna was my equal and, dare I admit it, a lot more. She lit up the stage. She took the town by storm, as in the years ahead she would take London by storm playing the title role in Shaw's *Saint Joan*. And I would be present to see that triumph also – a story to be told in its proper time.

After my success as a king, I looked forward to another leading part the following year. I didn't get one. I was back in the chorus, nursing my wounded pride. I even considered playing sick at the last moment, and might have tried it on had not something happened that would be of great importance not only to the school opera but to myself as well – the arrival of a new headmaster. Without warning he breezed into the classroom. 'I'm the new boss,' he announced and, in large letters, wrote COUGHLAN on the blackboard. 'That's my name. Caw-lan not Cock-lan. The initials are W.G.' And out he went as jauntily as he had entered. Such free-and-easiness was not expected from a Christian Brother, least of all from a Brother Superior.

W.G. preferred to guide, not drive. The strap, the pointer and bruising knuckles no longer ruled the classroom. If a student must be punished, W.G. administered the punishment himself in the privacy of his study, removed from gloating classroom eyes. 'Fifth-year students are not boys,' was his philosophy; 'they are young men.' He stopped not only the school but the town in its tracks when he insisted that the lay teachers wear gowns. Swank, some said. Ideas above his station. But gradually his students learned that W.G.'s ideas went far beyond a razor and polished shoes. He aimed to instil self-confidence into boys inured to playing second fiddle to the reputation of prominent boarding schools.

With a burst of his usual energy he raised the standard of the annual opera. Before his arrival, it had scrambled on stage under-rehearsed and hoping for the best, a ritual touch of the forelock to some vague curricular idea of culture. W.G. changed all that. Adequate time was given to rehearsal. There was no dodging, no horseplay behind the music teacher's back. A few days before the performance, classwork was set aside and rehearsals moved to St Macartan's Hall. The opera, W.G. made clear, was more than a doss. The prestige of the school was at stake.

When I entered St Macartan's for rehearsal, W.G. was on the stage in his shirt sleeves helping to erect the scenery. (Who had ever seen a Christian Brother in shirt sleeves?) The tattered woodland wings, for so long the dismal background to *céilidh* dancing, jumble sales and concerts in aid of parish funds, had been replaced by the deck of a ship, rails, bridge, helm and mast. Here was a setting to believe in. Here was an excitement no academic subject ever gave me.

The title of the opera was *Columbus in a Merry Key*, a title I thought very witty at the time. I was one of a chorus of Savants dispatched by Isabella of Castile to sail with Columbus on his journey to the New World. We were a grumpy lot who never found our sea legs. Our big moment came when the ship ran into a storm.

Clutching our stomachs we wailed our chorus of distress:

> *The horrible sea prevails and brandy and soda fails*
> *Misaree, misaree, misaree*

Overacting is easy – as John Stevenson, a radio director, was wont to say when an actor went over the top, 'Don't dip you bread in it.' I enjoyed dipping my bread in it. On opening night I clutched my stomach, I pulled faces, I threatened to vomit over the front row. Belly laughs were my reward. They went to my head and my staggering and vomiting became even more exaggerated on the second night. How far I would have gone on the third I dread to think had not W.G. wagged a finger and pointed out that comedy draws a clear line between amusing an audience and upsetting them. I was taken aback, especially because the criticism had come from him. But the acting bug had bitten me. If only faintly, I had heard the siren song.

My youth was a round of school, home exercises, exams, football, tennis in the summer, lazy holidays, winter lamplight and the wireless, money for the Saturday matinee, and home before dark. I was reared in a time of obedience, not of liberty, a time when people looked for and took direction from the Catholic Church. My parents allowed no slacking. It was morning and night prayers, Sunday mass and the sacraments. Lent was morning mass and communion in a freezing church – offer it up. It was fasting – one full meal and two collations (I enjoyed the word if not the meagre plate) – offer it up. It was abstain from meat on Wednesdays and Fridays – offer it up. Above all it was self-denial. I tried taking a cold bath, and sleeping with a book under my head instead of a pillow, but I was not made of the stuff of martyrs and settled for giving up sweets.

Religious instruction emphasised sanctity and sin – mostly sin.

I can still rattle off the Seven Deadly Sins, but if I imagined that they were of equal magnitude, I soon discovered that they fell into different categories of gravity. Covetousness was scarcely considered. Pride, Envy and Anger could easily be justified, and Sloth was the sin of the working class. Gluttony – drinking one's self and one's family out of house and home – was a serious but understandable frailty, a good man's fault. The remaining sin, Lust, was the sin of sins, the sin that put all others in the shade. In a darkened church Missionaries thundered about Purity, scaring the living daylights out of sinners young and old. Lust was the rat behind the wainscot: it gnawed at the burgeoning hormones of youth, it burrowed behind closed doors, in country lanes, and in the secrecy of bedrooms when the candle was extinguished. Lust ruled the lives of adolescent youth. There was no escape.

Touring actors, ever on the move from town to town, were 'the circus crowd', feckless and irresponsible, fugitives from a proper job. They lodged over pubs or on the working-class side of town. They trailed unfortunate children from one tatty lodging house to the next. Some couples, it was suspected, were not even married. They were a breed apart, curiosities, as freakish as foreigners.

Small companies won little kudos. Not so the Abbey. A 1930s' Abbey tour included Monaghan. The town was respectful, even more respectful than for Anew McMaster. Hadn't the Abbey visited America and gained international prestige? Weren't the actors respectable civil servants and insurance people? How fashionably the ladies dressed. The players attended mass on Sunday. Barry Fitzgerald and Sara Allgood, one-time members of the company, were regulars in films, as was Una O'Connor, greatly admired by my mother because she had turned down a Hollywood part she considered immoral.

With my mother I attended a performance of *The Far-Off Hills* by Lennox Robinson. Snatches remain: Patrick guided into the sitting room on his return from Dublin following a cataract operation; Pierce breaking down the reserve of Marian; Ducky and Pet chatting in bed about novels and boys. Homely stuff. No Shakespearean kings and queens, no melodrama villains. I hadn't realised that plays were written about ordinary people who led ordinary lives.

For me the actors were beings from another world. I couldn't believe that within a few years I would work with some of them and become friends with others. That impressive leading actress Eithne Dunne was one, Gerard Healy another. He would write *Thy Dear Father*, a long-runner in the Abbey, and *The Black Stranger*, a commemoration of the Famine, staged in the Gate in 1947. Other members of the company were Shela Ward, who managed Equity Productions, the first company I would join, and Fred Johnson who would become a friend and golfing partner. Most of all I remember Phyllis Ryan, founder and manager of Gemini Productions, the most successful independent company of the 1960s and '70s, for whom I would direct for twenty years and who would become a lifelong friend.

After the performance Lennox Robinson delivered a curtain speech. I had never before seen a writer in the flesh and expected a demigod with flowing locks – a Shelley or a Byron. Lennox did not fall into that category; he drooped like a weeping willow. His lank hair sagged over his nose. His trousers were at half-mast, one leg shorter than the other. He dangled over the footlights, long tapering hands flapping like a heron at take-off. His voice had the languorous quaver of a Church of Ireland pulpit. No one remembered what he said but everyone remembered what he looked like. 'The artistic temperament' was how my mother explained him away.

I was seventeen when the local dramatic society knocked on my door. The play was *The Lord Mayor*. The producer, as a director was called at the time, was the local curate. Not that he knew anything about drama; his job was to keep an eye on things. He needn't have worried about me. Playing opposite me was an attractive young lady, and of course our characters fell in love. And, of course, they kissed. In the script, that is. We didn't. Not properly. It wasn't any shyness on the girl's part but that, as we embraced, over the girl's shoulder, there, in the third row, was the glint of my mother's spectacles. I tried to back off. But the young lady hung grimly on and the audience were treated to a singular tug-o'-love with six inches of God's clean air between us.

Later, when we performed the play in a country hall far from my mother's glasses, I was a willing student of the young lady's tuition. (Which reminds me of a later encounter when, on a first night, an enthusiastic young actress took me off guard in our love scene by sticking her tongue halfway down my throat. By then, however, I was better fitted to deal with life's exigencies and my response was suitable to the occasion.)

If I had my problems in *The Lord Mayor*, what of our leading man, Bert, once a touring actor, now manager of a local cinema? Learning lines was not his forte. Close to the performance, his grasp on his dialogue was so sketchy that even our placid producer was worried. 'Relax,' Bert told him. He had it all planned. He would leave the script on the Lord Mayor's desk and use it when necessary.

'But the audience will know you're reading.'

'Not at all. Wait and see.'

We waited, and at the dress rehearsal we saw. Distributed amongst the documents on the Lord Mayor's desk were pages of script, letters arriving in the mail were copies of the text, when he lifted a corner of the hearth rug as if to remonstrate with a cleaner about how carelessly the room had been swept, underneath were prompts for a tricky speech written large enough to be read from a standing position. All of which are tricks of the trade I have seen used under stress when rehearsal time was short or memory overtaxed, but never have I seen anything like the final rabbit Bert pulled out of his inventive hat.

Standing at his desk, he called to the producer down the hall, 'Tell me, would you know I am reading?' and, leaning over the script, he lowered his eyelids. On each lid, drawn in greasepaint, was a staring eye that winked on and off like the beam of a lighthouse. The effect, like the jerky movements of a neon girl advertising a strip show, was mesmerising.

The first night came. Bert pattered from one treasure-trove of script to the next, his winking eyelids like beacons in a storm-tossed sea. Never had an audience seen the like. After the initial shock they settled down and when the final curtain fell Bert took his bow in triumph. 'I told you,' he said; 'they didn't notice a thing.'

I prepared for the Leaving Cert with a year of determined study. Hard work, my parents believed, was the recipe for a secure future. Too much brain power was distrusted. They reminded me of the boy who got First-Class Honours and suffered a nervous breakdown, and of eccentrics, especially mathematicians and philosophers, who wore odd socks and couldn't boil an egg. I courted the solitary room, facts and figures, index and glossary. I refrained from the cinema 'even for a break'. After tea, I worked into the small hours.

My only relaxation from this regime was when a touring company of English actors (who knows but that they were ducking conscription across the water?) played a rep of comedies and thrillers in the local town hall. *On the Spot* by Edgar Wallace was a big draw – who now remembers the name of the most successful thriller writer of his day? – gangsters in black shirts and white ties, the bulge of revolvers in inner pockets, actresses in clinging silk and plunging necklines. For days I chewed gum, drooped a fag from the corner of my mouth, fingered my gat and encircled the waist of my slinky moll. More fun than Shakespeare any day.

The company stage manager was over six feet tall and of fine physique, his long hair blowing in the breeze. On the morning the company was departing, I hung around The Diamond watching him oversee the loading of a lorry with the company scenery. When all was aboard, he did not climb into the cab with the driver but stretched full-length along the tailboard among stacked flats and theatrical skips. Watching him drive away, I remembered that other tall man, Lennox Robinson, his elegant hands fluttering like summer butterflies over the heads of a bemused audience. I could not imagine my father, or his friends, as carelessly dressed as Lennox or travelling, with mock stateliness, reclining along the tailboard of a truck weighed down by theatrical scenery. These men of the theatre were different from the burghers of my town, and that difference attracted me. I saw no absurdity in them as others did. I had begun to recognise my kin.

I worked diligently for the Leaving Certificate, spurred on not by dreams of a lustrous academic future but by a determination to be done with school. Latin was my weakest subject. To prepare me for the examination, P. J. Coleman, newly evacuated to Monaghan after the bombing of Belfast, was engaged to give me a grind. With him came a whiff of war, real war.

Ireland's war was shortages, ration books, trains labouring about the country fuelled by turf and chopped-up railway sleepers or anything combustible to keep the engines steaming. Motorcars crawled about, some weighed down by gas tanks to eke out rationed petrol. A quaint sight was the family saloon pottering along with a great balloon of gas on the roof flapping in the breeze like a deflated zeppelin.

In retrospect, it is extraordinary to have been so close to a vast conflict and simultaneously removed from it. Our war was arrows on a map indicating advances and retreats; it was everyone to attention around the wireless when Churchill rallied his faltering nation. It was Lord Haw-Haw flaying the Allies until my father flew into a rage. 'We beat the Hun in '18,' he declared, 'and we'll beat him again.' Even after Dunkirk he did not lose faith.

The bombing of Belfast brought other evacuees to Monaghan. With them came the reality of a conflict from which Ireland had stood aside. I have a poignant memory of a little Belfast girl who cried out in fear when she heard the sound of an approaching train, mistaking it for an aeroplane. 'The Germans are coming to bomb us again!' she screamed, and went on screaming until women came to comfort her.

If I had lived in England I would have been conscripted by the time I did my Leaving Cert. I had no wish to be a war hero. The book of First World War photographs in my father's desk told me all I wanted to know about war – and one in particular, that of a hand clutching the barbed wire entanglement. Attached to the hand was a forearm and a torn uniform sleeve, nothing more. In the background was a skeleton tree and the deathly, muddy void of No Man's Land. The hand was neither heroic nor defiant. It was no more than a dismembered hand – all that remained of a dead soldier blown to pieces on the barbed wire. For others the glory. Not for me.

Near the end of term it was announced that a prize would be awarded to the student who had worked most diligently throughout the year. Not to the most brilliant, but to the hardest worker. I knew I must be in with a chance because no other idiot thought it necessary to swot into the small hours and have enough study under his belt by Christmas to have passed a dozen exams. The prize was a Parker Pen. I won, but I did not fool myself that my success was for scholarship. I had won for keeping my nose to the grindstone. Sometimes that little success comes to mind when I read about a footballer who is voted the team's most valuable player. I can see him, steady, reliable, he doesn't make mistakes that cost a goal. He's no George Best but there will always be a place for him in the side. In time he will be in line for a testimonial. A Parker Pen perhaps.

A few weeks before the exam, my father was transferred to Mullingar, but it was thought best for the family not to move immediately so that my studies would not be interrupted. Before his departure my future was planned – I would go to university and take a degree. None of my sisters complained that I was the only member of the family destined for a university career. Being girls, they were not considered for a university education. They were women. Before marriage, they would work, as nurses, behind counters or in the civil service. After marriage, they would love, honour and obey their husbands and bear children, but I would be a doctor or a solicitor or an engineer or an architect – the choice was mine.

Around the age of twelve, thoughts of the church had briefly flamed when a visiting priest, recruiting for the foreign missions, appealed for volunteers to serve, in his haunting phrase, 'on the slopes of Kilimanjaro'. Instantly there rose a lump in my throat and the vision of sweating bodies in the sweltering heat, of Faith of Our Fathers soaring from grass huts and native bearers ferrying me, like Damien the Leper, from one mission station to the next. My ecstasy lasted for two days and that was the end of it.

I hadn't the faintest idea what I wanted to do when I left school. Medicine was out of the question because I was too squeamish for gore; poor mathematics ruled out engineering or architecture. But when I said I would like to study English, no one was pleased because it would qualify me for nothing but teaching, good enough for scholarship boys but not good enough for the son of the postmaster. Going on the stage did not even cross my mind. Acting was not a proper job.

After endless discussions with my father, my mother, my aunts and my uncles and Uncle Tom Cobley and all, I agreed to be a dentist, for no better reason than I found open mouths less repellent that sliced stomachs. That decided, I put my professional future out of mind and prepared for the Leaving Certificate. On the morning of the exam I arrived with my Parker Pen loaded and ready for action. I suffered no nervousness. The modern battle for points had not yet begun and I was confident that I would easily secure the couple of honours necessary for entry to the National University of Ireland.

When the last paper was handed up, I paused at the top of the school steps and told myself that I would never have to go to school again. But if I expected a trumpet call to herald my entry into the adult world, nothing happened. I walked down the steps and into the kitchen. I threw my books in a corner. Mother was working at the sink. 'Pick them up,' she said. 'Some poor child might be glad of them next year.'

2

It was decided that I would attend University College Cork. My parents came south to see me settled in. I was lodged in Glasheen Road; a few doors up lived Aunt Florrie; a few doors down lived Aunt Kathleen. An uncle resided in Tivoli and an aunt in Cross Douglas Road. All were members of my mother's family. They would look after me, she said. I didn't doubt it.

My landlady was Nellie, or Mrs Cremin to her student lodgers. She was small and plump with a single protruding tooth where her upper set had been. Her sitting room bore the scars of long student tenancy: shaky chairs, a cracked mirror, and dust. Dust everywhere, like a skim of desert sand. A tap on the table cover raised a grey plume of dust, a slap with an open hand left the imprint of thumb and forefinger. It was not that Nellie did not work hard – she never stopped –

but like those who lodged with her she was oblivious to the fine grey shroud that enfolded the family silver, the Infant of Prague, and the Papal Blessing.

Nellie sang in her kitchen and mothered her students. Forever she peeped from the front window to see if Bill, her husband, was coming down the road. 'He's retired,' she confided. 'Retired these few years.' At eleven in the morning she decked him in his trilby and gabardine raincoat and despatched him to the shops. After lunch he took a bus to the city and returned with the *Echo* in his pocket. He was an expert on newspaper puzzles that would win a five-pound fortune, on bus conductors who allowed him to travel on a nod and a wink, on who hurled top o' the left for Finbarrs, and on my relations, seed, breed and generation: my grandfather, 'a gentleman if ever there was one'; my uncle 'the best doctor in Cork'; the cousin who joined the Jesuits; and Uncle Dan who lived like a lord, rubber planting in Malaya. He even mentioned the unmentionable, Aunt Dot, who all those years before had decamped with a married man and in those straight-laced, unforgiving times, never darkened the family door again. Listening to Bill, I suspected that my parents had not accompanied me to Cork to see me settled into a city but into a big small town.

In digs with me were two medical students: Liam, a Munster lock forward, and Sean, with two repeated years behind him. Liam gave me advice: 'Never miss a lecture. Take plenty of notes. A month before the exam, revise like a hoor. The rest of the time you can arse around all you like.'

'All right for him,' Sean said. 'Never stuck an exam. Friggin' honours, too.'

I decided that I, too, would get honours. I would study like a hoor and in my final year some impressionable First Year would look at me and think, 'Honours. Friggin' honours.'

Exalted by dreams of academic distinction, I laid out my textbooks and pinned a work schedule to the wall. But I couldn't work. I tried and failed. Tried again and failed again. Every day I vowed to start tomorrow, every weekend that I would begin for sure on Monday. I prayed. I fingered the fountain pen that only a few months previously was my reward for application, but by the end of term I was drifting on a tide of novels and films and inactivity, my dream of honours, friggin' honours swiftly fading.

I stayed in Cork over Christmas. My father had not yet found a suitable house in Mullingar and the family's departure from Monaghan was delayed. I drifted from picture house to bookshop, killing time. Everyman Classics gathered on my bedside table concealing unopened textbooks. If the author's name was venerable, I purchased the volume and laboured pretentiously with Carlyle and Ruskin when I could have relaxed with a bestseller. I read into the small hours, indifferent to my bleary-eyed next morning when I would stare from Nellie's window hoping for a miracle that would release me from my lassitude.

Astoundingly, it happened. In the middle of the day, slap bang, just like that. I was crossing the university quadrangle when the still, small voice that had whispered during a school operetta gave tongue in tones that were loud and clear. *You won't be a dentist*, it said. *You will tread the boards and posture in the spotlight's beam.*

I walked on water. I bestrode the universe. Confident that my parents would be equally elated by my decision, I wrote home. Florid phrases flowed from my pen in what seemed to be a masterpiece of emotional expression. I even thought of saving a copy for my autobiography. In reply I expected a letter and not that, two days later, my parents would knock on Nellie's door. The interview that followed was painful. My mother remained silent. My father asked the questions. How did I expect to make a decent living on the stage? Had I not seen poor divils of show-people dragging around the country without a sole to their shoes or a rag on their backs? Would I have a pension to retire on?

In the early 1940s (indeed, even now) 'going on the stage' was not a proper job. Drop-outs, eccentrics or ne'er-do-wells might join a travelling show or a circus, with its smell of horse dung, clowns, and flaunting women attired in tights, but it was ordained that the middle class, to which I belonged, would fill the ranks of the professions.

Discussions lasted for three days, after which I agreed to remain in college until the end of the academic year. I did not see the point, but it seemed a small sacrifice to please my parents. A few months, that was all, and I would be on my way.

I bought two-tone shoes. My hair was a helmet of solid Brylcreem. From the side of my mouth drooped a permanent cigarette and, when James Cagney was not my style, a cigarette holder paid homage to Noël Coward. I attended lectures only to attract attention and joined the Dramatic Society because I thought it would be a step in the right direction.

Bill, the ever vigilant, the all-knowing, had not missed a trick. Like the Ancient Mariner, he buttonholed me to recount the woeful histories of students who had left college without a degree. Wasters, they were, who broke their mother's hearts, fit for nothing but Kilburn and the pick and shovel.

To give weight to his words, he produced a Christmas-present cigar and punctuated his homily with puffs of smoke, tapping the ash into a saucer he carried in his left hand. When his tale was told, he topped the cigar with a broken-bladed scouting knife and the saucer of ash, protected from wind and weather by a cupped hand, was carried from the room. More homilies followed, at the climax of each, when another waster bit the dust, the cigar was topped and another inch added to the growing snail of ash.

What was so precious about cigar ash? I wondered.

'For the teeth. Nothing like cigar ash for polishing the teeth.'

Depositing the saucer of ash on the centre of the table, 'Your grinders could do with a bit of a scrub' was his parting shot.

The ash haunted me. Why I didn't throw it in the fire and pretend I'd used it I don't know, but I didn't. Every day I stared at it like a rabbit hypnotised by a weasel. It was only when Bill started on about wasters who fell by the wayside, in the dubious life of the theatre, that a thought came to me and, waiting for him to leave the room, I steeled myself, took my stance at the table and squared-up to the saucer and its heap of ash. It was me or it. No quarter.

Filling my lungs I let it have it. The result was a Bikini Atoll of ash that spread its mushroom cloud over the dining table, the Infant of Prague, the family silver and the Papal Blessing. Not a speck of ash remained. The Alien was vaporised.

Next day Bill was suspicious. 'Did you use that ash?' he asked me.

'No. It blew away.'

He got the message, picked up the empty saucer, and retired in a sulk to the kitchen. And that was the last I heard of student wasters.

Thirst, a one-act comedy by Myles na gCopaleen was the Dramatic Society's contribution to the Annual Rag Revue. Cork's leading director, James Stack, produced, and I played one of the drinkers in the pub. It was my first time on stage since I had made my Great Decision and every detail should be crystal clear in my memory, the way it is in the best theatre autobiographies, but all I remember is sitting on a barstool, spotlights beaming down, and the fleshy blur of faces out front. Crystal clear is the aftermath. I could not slow down. In the dressing room, bottles were lined up. A teacup filled with whiskey was thrust into my hand – 'Drink it, son, it's only *yalla wather.*' I did, and asked for more. And kept it down. God knows how much I drank. And stayed upright. Beginner's luck.

The night zoomed. On the Western Road dustbin lids bit the dust. Nearing home, companions dropped off, bosom pals, friends for life, hard men, until, content in my own company, I trod the centre of Glasheen Road exulting to the moon or stars or whatever was up there that a life in the theatre lay ahead and soon my troubles would be over.

Far from it. Arriving home at the end of term, I believed that my university career had ended but, before I knew where I was, a prospectus tumbled through the letterbox and discussions proceeded about finding a different course for next year, something I would find more appealing than dentistry. I would not return to Cork. I would attend University College Dublin. A fresh start.

I agreed. God knows why. Lack of resolution; a habit of obedience; perhaps a secret desire to win my parents' approval before going on to fame and fortune with their benediction on my head. And so the summer passed while I strode about the drawing room declaiming Wilde and Marlowe, textbook in hand, like Oliver Goldsmith at the gates of Trinity.

Accommodation in Dublin was arranged in the De La Salle Hostel in Ely Place, nicknamed Ding Dong because of the thunderous hand bell that summoned students to meals in the basement refectory. The hostel was an extension of boarding school, the Brothers' strict regime a reassurance for parents who feared for the virtue of sons loosed from the apron strings. A Sacred Heart lamp burned in the hallway before a statue of Christ the King. The front door was locked at eleven. Breakfast at eight, dinner at one, tea at six. Giant pots of tea, milk and sugar already added. A fried egg congealed on a plate. Jacket potatoes hurled by frolicsome students to splatter on the walls. Visitors in the parlour. Cosy chats with Brother Superior about how the work was going – not very well, as far as I was concerned.

There were the diligent students, among them Paddy O'Keeffe who would edit *The Irish Farmers Journal* and Tom (Thomas P.) O'Neill, who would become a distinguished historian and official biographer of Eamon de Valera.

Not all the students were models of decorum. Five nights a week Reily (let's call him that) was drunk and truculent. When challenged by Brother Superior, he hurled a china ewer through a closed window to shatter four floors below in Ely Place. Once, late at night, he knocked on my door. 'Come on for a steak.'

'I've no money.'

'For fuck sake, I have.'

He had smouldering eyes. He walked with his head down. In Stephen's Green he windmilled a bottle of stout high in the air to fall and explode like a bomb opposite the Shelbourne Hotel.

The Green Rooster was a late night restaurant in O'Connell Street. A manager with suspicious eyes missed nothing. A chucker-out kept an eye on Reily and Reily kept an eye on the chucker-out. When he tried to slip out without paying, a barrel chest and closed fists barred his way. Without protest he paid up from a wallet stuffed with notes. I wanted to know why he tried to get out without paying? 'Fuckers,' was his only answer.

Why Reily choose me as a companion, I don't know. Why I joined him, I don't know. Curiosity, I suppose, and a fascination with his simmering violence and undisguised unhappiness. Late at night, wearing only a shirt, he shook me awake. 'Come on.'

'What's up?'

'Fuck you. Come on.'

On the landing outside his room stood a pallid woman. Her threadbare coat hung loose. 'Get the hoor out,' he said to me.

'You didn't pay me,' the woman said.

'Fuck off,' said Reily.

In the half-light everything was surreal; Reily naked but for his shirt, myself half-asleep and an ageing prostitute on the top floor of a hostel run by Christian Brothers.

I led the woman down the stairs. When we were two flights down, a venomous whisper came from above, 'Syphilis. Filthy hoor.'

The woman looked up at the piercing eyes that stared down at her. 'Mean bastard. You didn't pay me.'

I hurried her on, fearful of black-uniformed celibates listening behind bedroom doors or waiting to confront me at the foot of the stairs. But only the red glow of the Sacred Heart lamp illuminated the polished floor of the gloomy hall and the beckoning statue of Christ the King.

The woman touched my arm. 'Ten bob.'

I held the hall door open.

'Five bob.'

I pulled away.

'Bastard. Mean bastard.'

The woman repelled me with her half-fed sallowness and suggestion of an existence fit only for the pages of low-life literature, a character from the underside of decency. Green adolescents, such as I was, sneered at prostitutes: whores, tarts and nymphos who enjoyed it. Steal your cash and give you the clap. I had no pity for the woman. Maturity would teach me that when I closed the door behind her, it was her appearance I shut out, not her wares.

Margo was different. I met her in a mid-town restaurant, no greasy-spoon haunt of pale bohemians and vociferous drunks, but a much-frequented restaurant where businessmen hung up their hats before reading the *Evening Herald*. She was in the company of Rory, a university student who stuck Third Med and stayed stuck. He had an angel face, blond hair and a melodious tenor voice. 'Join us,' he said. I did, surprised to find him escorting such glamour, for Margo had B-movie glitz. She was lush, she wore a fur coat, her hair was dyed blonde. We chatted – or rather Rory and I chatted while Margo sipped her coffee until, with a 'Talk to Margo,' Rory left us to it.

Conversation with Margo was limited. 'Would you like a cigarette?' 'Thanks.' That was it. Her eyes followed Rory's progress from table to table. Here and there he paused for a word with a man sitting on his own or for an exchange that drew glances in Margo's direction.

With a deafening clang, the penny dropped. I was in a public restaurant sharing coffee with a prostitute, and Rory was her pimp. Far from feeling shamed I felt daring, a man of the world, an actor storing up copy. Margo was no furtive creature seen in the half-light of a religious-run institution; this was a businesswoman plying her trade. At a nod from Rory she drew her fur coat around her and left the restaurant with a flourish.

Being a friend of the management, so to speak, Rory made me a special offer – cut price, the selling point a graphic run-down of Margo's versatility. Have you never done it? You'd like it. She's nice.

She'd help. I refused, not expecting to hear the beat of angel wings at my back but because I was in dread of syphilis and the roaring flames of Hell that sent shivers down the spine of hot-blooded youth. Or did when I was young. Nowadays we hear very little about Hell. Like an overage matinee idol, Hell has faded from the scene.

Why did I view Margo differently from the dejected creature on the stairs of Ding Dong? Because Margo was glamorous? Because she wore a fur coat? My brush with her knocked some of the prudery out of me, but I would have to do a lot of growing up before I understood that snobbery had shaped my moral code.

My frustration at wasting another year in university turned into resentment against my parents. Unreasonably, I blamed them for impeding my progress towards the theatre. Self-pity is a comfortable funk-hole; I pined for the theatre but did nothing about it. Except once.

On impulse I wrote to Lord Longford at the Gate Theatre requesting an interview. A few days later a reply summoned me to the Gaiety, where Longford Productions was performing.

Lord Longford was a large, overweight man, remembered by his generation at the theatre exit rattling a collection box in aid of theatre funds. He was friendly, if a little nervous, and always courteous. He questioned me about my age, my experience, and asked if I was interested in joining the professional theatre.

'Yes, Lord Longford.'

'Then I suppose you'd better do something for me.'

I had come prepared – the great speech from Marlowe's *Doctor Faustus* no less. I would impress. I would make an impact. Not for nothing had I shaken the walls of the drawing room in Mullingar when the house was empty. Facing Lord Longford, I filled my lungs and let rip like an overcharged fairground barker, 'Is this the face that launched a thousand ships—'

Lord Longford shifted uneasily. 'There's no need to speak so loudly. There are only two of us in the room.'

And I thought I'd got off to a flying start.

I tried again. What emerged was the rasping of a medium in a trance. I thought the speech would never end. At last I got there – the Devil will come and Faustus will be damned.

A long silence.

Lord Longford cleared his throat. 'I don't remember anyone doing *Faustus*.' Pause. 'No one.' Pause. 'Never.'

Silence.

'And you want to be a professional actor?'

'Yes, Lord Longford.'

'Ah ha . . . I see . . . Ah ha.'

'Would you like me to do another piece?'

In an instant Lord Longford was on his feet. 'The curtain is coming down. I must go backstage. Thank you, thank you.'

The backstage stairs in the Gaiety are stone and cheerless. Halfway down I glanced back. Lord Longford was in the dressing room door, gazing after me. Our eyes met. He fled for cover.

My academic career in UCD was simple: missed lectures, time-wasting, the dramatic society, and not even the pretence of working. I have forgotten how I came to play a part in a production in the Eccles Street convent. Someone roped me in, I suppose. The director, Maura

Cranny, was a lady of common sense who decided that, even in a convent, the male parts should be played by men and not girls with grease-paint moustaches and bulging shirtfronts.

The play was *The Admirable Crichton* by J. M. Barrie. In the cast were young women from the convent, or who had attended it, and their dragged-in male friends, including Brendan Cauldwell, who would progress to the theatre, the Radio Éireann Repertory Company and, notably, *Fair City*.

The Admirable Crichton was given three performances. I played the title role, lapping up the applause that came my way. Critical or uncritical, polite hand-clapping or standing ovation, applause is the lifeblood of the performer. Someone, that witty man David Kelly, I believe, remarked that from the time an actor gets out of bed in the morning he is waiting in the wings for his entrance.

Tea and sandwiches and polite conversation with the nuns delayed me after the performance on the first couple of nights. And when the rest of the cast were heading for coffee in the Savoy, I was legging it to Ding Dong before the hall door was bolted at eleven. For the last night I requested a door key and permission to stay out after curfew.

Brother Superior was a pallid man with a voice of trip-wire smoothness. 'At what time will the play finish?'

'About ten or so.'

'And the door here will not be locked until eleven.'

It was the last night I explained. After the play I would like to join my friends for coffee.

'Coffee. Yeeees.' And how would I get home?

Last bus. Or walk.

'Walk. Yeeees.' And would I walk alone?

'Some of the men in the cast will be with me most of the way.'

'And the young ladies?'

Suddenly I was a late night, alcoholic rapist.

'No key,' he said. The door would remain open until twelve and not a moment longer. That was it. Take it or leave it.

After the play there was supper and a goodbye to the nuns. Restaurants were closing by the time we left the convent but spirits were too high to go tamely home. Someone knew a back-street all-night café. It was getting late but I'd risk it. The talk, like all good talk, went on too long and suddenly it was midnight. Cinderella time, glass slipper time. I ran all the way to Ding Dong. Every window was black. I knocked and waited. Knocked again. Not a face peered down from a window. Not a censorious Brother came down to let me in. Not a virtuous curfew-abiding, mother's-pride-and-joy deigned to open the door. Not a sneak-in-half-jarred-and-puke-in-the-jax old lag came to my rescue.

In an alleyway at the back of the building was a wall that could be scaled by grabbing an iron frame that once housed a gas lamp. Swinging up and over, I dropped into the back garden. The kitchen door was locked. So were the basement windows. I whistled and called, not caring any longer what reprimand awaited me if only I got in. Never before had I been locked out of anywhere. Thieves, marauders and drunks were locked out. They had given cause and earned exclusion, but I had done no more than let time slip and missed a childish curfew. Momentarily I glimpsed the face of a Brother looking down from a window on the second floor but he did not descend to open the door.

I turned to the billiard room, a decaying adjunct to the house, a hint of past affluence hung with spiders' webs like an apartment in Miss Havisham's time-stopped mansion. Dust was everywhere; on the peeling table, on the scoreboard that read 50 – 33, on two cues and a broken one, on a three-legged chair that tipped over when I sat on it.

Cursing my world and those who ran it, I lay on the table and tried to sleep. Not a hope. I saw the night through until the first rays of dawn. Then I took stock of the absurdity of my situation. Here I was, stretched on a billiards table, the cloth wrapped around me, locking eyes with a framed Robert Emmet who hung on the wall, heroic in his green and glory uniform. My mind reverted to school and the strap, to parents and teachers and a list of secular and religious guardians of my faith and morals. I had no urge to upend the world, to rape or pillage or run naked through the streets, but if I did not soon do something about it, others would run my life forever.

I rose from the table, picked up a cue and stood eye to eye with Robert Emmet, national hero. The distance was right. I took aim and lunged. The glass splintered, and the hero was impaled by a javelin through the heart. I climbed back over the wall and dropped into Baggot Street. The sun was up. I ran, flapping my arms. I had wasted enough time trying to please everyone.

Parting with the academic world, I decided that to fail gloriously would be a suitable farewell. I sat the exam, sucked my pen, and was an alien among the swots who would confidently open the university envelope when their results dropped through the letterbox. When mine arrived, my father cast a pained look over them and left the room without a word.

Another summer drifted past, while I did no more about my future than chuck stones at an empty cigarette box floating on the canal where I walked with my sister Toni. 'Are you certain you want to be an actor?' was her searching question.

'I'm certain.'

'Then that's what you must be.'

Toni was ten years older than me, a woman of style and reserve that could be mistaken for haughtiness. Too much of a lady, my father snapped, when there were words between them, which there often were. Bouts of depression regularly troubled my father and, when they struck, his family suffered from his moroseness and his anger. He did not set out to hurt, of that I am sure, but those of his febrile temperament are so destructive in the close confines of family life that they inflict wounds that may take a heavy toll in later years. All his family suffered but we kept things to ourselves, behind lace curtains and, sadly, were relieved when the time came to leave home.

Thoughts of the theatre occupied my days and nights. I had no idea how to get started professionally, but luck was on my side when I spotted a newspaper advertisement for a school of acting to be run in the Gaiety Theatre under the guidance of the Abbey actress Ria Mooney. My father was non-committal when I said I had applied, but he wished me good luck when I was called for interview.

My interview was surprisingly brief. Did I want to be a professional actor or to do the course for fun? To be a professional, Miss Mooney. And I wanted to study production. 'Ah,' Ria said, 'I have only a few who want to be producers.' An encouraging remark, but I went home not daring to hope.

After a couple of anxious weeks, word arrived that I had been accepted. My father was resigned. 'If the theatre is what you want,' he said, 'your mother and I won't stand in your way. I would have supported you until you got a degree in the university, I will support you for the same length of time until you get on your feet.' No more generous offer could be made by a parent who must have felt let down.

It could not have been easy for my parents. They were convention-al people sure of their place in small town society in a time when loose-living Hollywood scandalised propriety, when films were cen-sored and a play could whistle up a storm of outrage. To have their only son abandon university for the uncertainties of the stage must have been the bitterest of pills. It is easy to look back and understand their disappointment, but at the time I gave the matter little thought. The theatre had called and I must answer.

The summer was one of buoyant days waiting for autumn and the school of acting to open. At last the day arrived when I was due to leave but, before I was on my way, a shock awaited. And from where I least expected it. My bag was packed, Toni was waiting to accompany me to the station, my father had wished me well. I turned to my moth-er to bid her goodbye. 'It's not our fault,' she said. 'Your father and I did our best.'

I was thunderstruck. My father tried to intervene but she went on, 'After all we did for him. Going around the country like a tinker.'

Since the first discussions in Cork about my wish to become an actor, I had taken for granted that my mother's silence indicated that she was on my side. Not for a moment had I suspected her disap-proval.

'I won't go!' I cried. 'I'll stay at home!' Dramatics. Even as I spoke I knew that to resist the call of the theatre would be a kind of suicide. Toni kept her head. Grabbing my suitcase, she dragged me from the kitchen. In the station she bought a Baby Power and stuffed it into my pocket. 'She'll get over it,' she said.

I knocked back the Baby Power and bought another on the train. When I reached Westland Row I was in the clouds. Grandly, I tipped a porter sixpence to carry my bags and walked ahead of him up the platform. At the barrier I handed over my one-way ticket, lit a cigarette and emerged into the city. I was on my way.

Ria Mooney was a gifted teacher and an actress of great ability. At Christmas, when she invited me to accompany her Christmas shopping with her little niece, I longed for the passing throng to take note that I was the companion of a distinguished woman. Her frankness took me by surprise when she mentioned casually, in a time when a woman's age was a dark secret, 'I'm forty-two.'

She introduced her students to a wide variety of playwrights – from Synge to Chekhov, to Molière to Wilde, and the styles required for each. Her course was not bound by set terms, it was ongoing: attend for as long as you like, stay for as long as you like, take what you wish from the course and move on. I attended for six months, a period much briefer than the two-year courses available nowadays, but I doubt if any student in one of today's drama schools gets a better grounding than I did under Ria's tuition.

Because acting was very much a pastime to be indulged outside commercial hours, and all but a few of the students had full-time jobs, classes did not commence until five in the evening. That left me with a lot of time on my hands. I pottered around art galleries, attended the theatre – back row in the Gate, the gods in the Abbey – and saw more films than I can remember. After class, it was coffee with fellow students in the Savoy in O'Connell Street, where Mme Van Aalst and her orchestra churned out requests from among the potted palms.

Another time-killer was to learn the geography of Dublin by boarding a bus to one suburb or another, and walking back. On my shelves is a photographic record of the city shot in the fifties by the painter Nevill Johnson. It recalls Dublin as I first knew it, a middle class of two-piece costumes and three-piece suits and, for the rest, black shawls and tattered jackets. It records the rundown grandeur of Georgian doorways hiding want within: the Herald Boot Fund appealing for subscriptions to shoe destitute children; hunger; TB. This was dear old dirty Dublin, down at heel, trams and horse-drawn drays, a place where men gave up their seats to ladies, where poverty was rife, where one walked home in safety after dark through the shortcuts and back alleys, where children went barefoot and the underclass knew its place.

Ria's production students had the privilege of attending rehearsals in the Theatre Royal. This was during the war when Cine-Variety was the weekly bill, a film showing three times daily, the showings separated by a one-hour variety show of comedy, music and dance. Potted thrillers were an added attraction, the dastardly deed and the villain unmasked all in ten minutes. Another series was 'Historical Vignettes' in one of which, *Committee Room 15 or The Downfall of Parnell*, a fellow student and myself were sent along by Ria to make up the numbers. We had a couple of lines each and at our first rehearsal were given simple instructions: 'Look for the nearest microphone, lads. And speak as loudly as you can.' No acting school nonsense in a theatre that held over three and a half thousand.

Walking on stage was like walking into an aircraft hangar. Amplification launched voices into the unknown and audience reaction returned like an echo from a well. This was my first professional engagement. I got two pounds ten shillings for the week, real wealth for a hard-up student but, what was more exciting, I rubbed shoulders with the performers who brought success to the theatre during the war years: the leading comic Noel Purcell, Jimmy Campbell and his orchestra, and the novelty of *Double or Nothing*, an onstage quiz compered by Eddie Byrne, the prize a half-note or a quid (ten shillings or a pound in old, very old, currency). Not quite *Who Wants to be a Millionaire?* but fun, when money was tight and people counted their loose change before buying a raffle ticket.

The dance team, The Royalettes, was choreographed by Alice Dalgarno, of whom I was in awe. No gentle tones were hers. I can still hear her belting out the timing, One, Two, Three, Four, One, Two, Three, Four, while the tap shoes hammer out the rhythm and I am dazzled by the flashing legs.

Comedy sketches were written by Dick Forbes. Week after week he produced a new script and managed a pantomime when Christmas came around. Little credit is given to script writers – comedians, singers and dancers are the visible part of a show, in the pit the conductor waves a baton, but how many give a thought to the writer who puts the words in the comic's mouth?

Over the theatre ruled T. R. Royal, a cover-name for the impresario Louis Elliman, also owner/manager of the Gaiety, known universally as 'Mister Louis'. Underlings like myself did not actually bow in his presence, but we thought about it. At the dress rehearsal he sat out front to vet the show. Comedy sketches, especially, attracted his attention. At the slightest hint of a double-meaning joke, his voice was raised – 'Cut.' No more, no less. Occasionally there was a plaintive protest of, 'Ah, Mister Louis.' A waste of time. 'Cut' was repeated and that was the end of it. His concern, I imagine, was governed not so much by prudishness as by the fact that the Royal attracted a family audience that must not be offended. Standards change, the boundaries are pushed, but the rule remains: offend the audience and they don't come back.

Huge settings were essential to dress the vast stage. Somewhere in the stratosphere, Fergus O'Farrell, and later Brian Collins, laboured on the paint frame, producing towering backcloths, or knocking up anything from an ocean liner to an iced cake from which fairies appeared to tap out a number, or a spunky soprano glittered in glossy flounces to thrill us with a high C. Production numbers transported us to exotic climes; Honolulu this week, Mexico next. May Devitt sang love duets with Joseph Locke and from a balcony the movie star Movita threw a rose to Jack Doyle.

Jack Doyle! Who remembers Jack Doyle, the Gorgeous Gael, a pop idol before pop idols were invented? He came to prominence as a boxing champion with the Irish Guards, and from there it was a professional boxing career, with bouts for the British Championship. He never won it, but he remained the Gorgeous Gael, the stuff that tabloids dream of, women trailing in his wake. His reputation filled the biggest arenas, with crowds baying for their money's worth and getting it. Fights finished early when haymakers knocked opponents out of the ring or they knocked Doyle out of it.

He had a fine tenor voice and in his glory days he filled the leading theatres in Britain. He even made a film, *McGlusky the Sea Rover*, that traded on his pop image, and I am reliably informed by a friend that he appeared in *The Bells of Saint Trinian's*, which must have been fun for the gymslips.

As rapidly as he climbed to fame, he slid down again. I have two memories of him, the first when his star had begun to fade. He was on a barstool in Davy Byrnes, drink in hand, surrounded by henchmen. He still looked pretty good. His hair – oh those glorious waves – had no tinge of grey, his physique was still impressive. My last memory of him is from a street near Notting Hill Gate, perhaps fifteen years later.

I recognised him at once, his shoulders were by now a little rounded but there was no mistaking the magnificent build. I followed him for a time, remembering the palmy days of listening to his fights on the wireless and seeing him star with Movita in the Theatre Royal, backed by an orchestra, dancing girls, palms and a blue, blue sea. By now he was knocking out a living singing in pubs, and Irish morality, which tagged along behind him when times were good, dismissed him, when his star began to fade, as a weakling who could not handle his fame. But following him on a street in London, I remembered that for a time he made it big, very big, and the best of luck to him.

There is a coda to my memories of Jack Doyle. For a time he was married to the film star Movita, one of her list of husbands which included Marlon Brando. She was popularly described as fiery. When she and Doyle toured Ireland with their own show, offstage action abounded, including, rumour had it, damage to the hotel in my local town, Balbriggan. If it was true, Balbriggan did not hold it against them and years later when the hotel was replaced by a fashionable, modern building, it included the Jack Doyle Lounge and the Movita Night Club. Remembering the rumpus caused years before by Doyle and Movita, I asked a barmaid jokingly, 'Who was Jack Doyle?' She considered for a moment before answering, 'Some fella from the town, I suppose.' That's fame for ya.

At the end of the school year came the student show, staged in the Gaiety. I have the programme still, found by accident when a drawer of odds and ends was upended to make a bonfire. Two performances were given, afternoon and evening. Two plays were performed, a full-length, *The Good Hope*, and a one-act comedy, *Crabbed Youth and*

Age. In the afternoon I played an old sailor in *The Good Hope* and in the evening appeared as an aspiring young playwright, Gerald, in *Crabbed Youth and Age.* Ria Mooney, who directed, whispered in my ear that the part of the young playwright was a smile at his youthful self by the author Lennox Robinson. Remembering his curtain speech when the Abbey visited Monaghan, I needed little encouragement to play the part with wafting hands and wavering tones. All of which was fun until the dressing room door opened after the show and Lennox peered in. Not for a moment had I expected him to attend, least of all to come backstage. Casting an eye around he picked me out, wagged a long finger and intoned, 'Naughty. Naughty.' Whether he was jesting or ticking me off, I didn't dare ask.

Many years later, when I was invited by an acquaintance to make up a four at bridge, I met Lennox formally. The evening was one of conversation rather than card-playing, with Lennox regaling the company with tales of Yeats and the early Abbey. None could have been more entertaining company. Not that he was always so benign. Friends who ran a drama school presented their students in *The Whiteheaded Boy* and sent Lennox a courtesy invitation, not expecting him to accept. When he did, I was asked along to keep him company, which meant inviting him across the road for a drink in the interval. After the show he came backstage to be introduced to the cast. He was at his most gracious, joking gleefully that, 'I wrote the play over a weekend and have lived on it ever since.'

After the usual courtesies, the actors retired to store away memories of a happy encounter with the great man. All but one. He hovered, attempting to engage Lennox in conversation, undeterred by the fact that he was being studiously ignored. Finally, plonking himself squarely in front of Lennox, he asked brashly, 'What did you think of it, Mr Robinson?' He was a small man, bald and tubby. Lennox was willowy-tall and slim. From his lofty elevation he peered down on his interlocutor. 'Oh,' he answered with devastating off-handedness, 'I enjoyed it. In spite of you.'

At an amateur drama festival one of Lennox's plays was on the boards. The adjudicator spotted him out front and, intending it as a compliment, commenced his adjudication by remarking that the company had given a very good performance of 'Lennox Robinson's charming little play.' From down the hall came a stern correction, 'I never wrote a little play.' Nor did he. Gentle plays, perhaps, but not little plays. His output was a mirror of the Ireland of his time, a prim middle-class Ireland now faded. He chronicled the everyday; he did not probe into the dark corners of the soul. His characters lived in small towns, as in *Church Street*, one of his early plays. Travelling from town to town on the business of the Carnegie Libraries, he knew his small towns intimately and turned on them his acute observation and affectionate good humour.

Not all his plays were small town comedies. He dealt with the vanishing ascendancy in *The Big House* and in *Killycreggs in Twilight*, but it was to his popular comedies that audiences turned. *The Whiteheaded Boy*, *The Far-Off Hills*, and *Drama at Inish* were evergreen Abbey revivals until some years after his death in 1958.

From the yellowing programme of that Gaiety School production two names stand out: Eamonn Andrews, a future star of television, and Milo O'Shea, already with a tour on the road behind him. In a few years he would head for America and make an impressive career on Broadway, but in drama school it was more his talent for comedy than his skills as an actor that caught the eye.

Another name that would become familiar was that of P. J. O'Connor, who would be the first to adapt *Tarry Flynn* for the Abbey, and, after a move into radio, be remembered for the P. J. O'Connor Radio Drama Awards. Nor have I overlooked the name of Cecil King, a painter and designer of subtle elegance.

Some names recall those who attended the school for fun but had no wish to enter the professional theatre – secretly I thought them traitors to the cause – and, inevitably, after the passage of years there are names that no longer have a face to give them an identity. And there are the sad names whose dearest wish was to make a professional career but who failed. Dedication is not enough; there is no substitute for talent.

Around this time I met a real actor, Edward Mulhare. I first saw him perform when I was attending University College Cork in a production of *Cradle Song* in the Cork Opera House. The action of the play unfolds in the convent of an enclosed order of nuns. Communication with the outside world is through a revolving grill in the main door. Through the grill arrives a baby in a crib to be cared for and raised by the nuns. In time the baby grows into a young woman and a suitor claims her hand. This was Edward; tall, handsome, golden-haired, with a voice that was full and resonant – perfect attributes for a matinee idol. And he knew it. When I invited him to the dress rehearsal of an amateur show I was directing in UCD, he draped himself in the front row, cigarette smoke curling from a languid hand. Female eyelids fluttered. An impressionable ingénue playing the maid dropped her duster and went to pieces when he returned it with a flashing smile.

The leading lady was bookish, and she acted her love scene with the stony resolve of a pilgrim at Lough Derg. When the final curtain came down, Edward summoned her to his presence. 'My dear girl,' he explained, 'an onstage kiss is no more than another piece of stage business,' and demonstrated by embracing her without warning and kissing her as I suspect she had never been kissed before. Purple-faced and speechless, she swept into the wings, leaving Edward to remark, 'Amateurs must learn to rid themselves of their inhibitions.'

Above all else, Edward was a performer, one for whom a script was no more than a vehicle to ply his actor's trade. Stardom was his vision and he was relentless in its pursuit.

To be a star a performer needs that touch of magic that singles him or her out from the crowd. Personality, charisma – call it what you like – stardom is a love affair between the performer and his audience. Stars are born. They have that extra something. Edward never doubted that he had it. In ten years, he declared, he would make it. It took a little longer than that, but I was around when his big break came.

My favourite memory of him is of an evening when I called to his digs. He was at the dining table, a copy of Shakespeare propped against the teapot, declaiming *Hamlet* to half a dozen assorted civil servants and shop assistants struggling with their sausages. Some were embarrassed, some amused, some derisive, but all had a glint of grudging admiration for his shameless exhibitionism. In a time of rationed food, patched clothes and under-powered light bulbs, in a lacklustre wartime world, Edward declaiming Shakespeare to sausages and fried bread injected a flash of colour into drab workaday lives. Perhaps he inspired a dream or two. Stars are the dreamsmiths of the dream factory.

While Edward was enlivening boarding house tea tables with readings from the Bard, I made my first acquaintance with studio theatre. A studio theatre was any small space adapted for the production of plays. Any space would suffice if the guiding force behind it had the enthusiasm to have a go.

The studio theatre was an outlet for new ideas and uncommercial scripts. It attracted the up-and-coming, the aspiring, the pretentious and those embittered by Abbey rejection slips. Audiences were often no more than a handful of dedicated aficionados and reluctant relations dragged along by the scruff of the neck. In basement or attic could be found unsmiling cohorts planning to bring life back to Dublin's flaccid theatre scene: the Gate company of Mac Liammóir and Edwards was stagey, Longford Productions were irrelevant and the Abbey had lost its way. Unpublished authors bulged with rejected scripts; intellectuals spoke reverently of Moscow.

Mme D. Bannard Cogley, 'Toto' to one and all, ran her studio theatre in South Anne Street. She was a diminutive, vibrant French woman, dedicated to the theatre and responsible for introducing a number of young actors to the Dublin stage. Her studio was a converted first-floor room where a full house numbered thirty hardy souls who settled for hotchpotch seating and an opportunity to see plays of quality ignored by the established theatres.

When I was introduced to her studio, Toto was working on three one-act plays, in one of which, *A Night of the Trojan War* by John Drinkwater, I was cast as a defender of Troy. Quoting rhyming couplets, I kept watch for approaching Persians by peering into the wings at a blank wall six inches from my nose. At curtain-fall I died a noble death.

During rehearsal the death scene worked well. I gave the cue, the Persian attacker leaped from a couple of beer crates concealed behind a canvas rock, we crossed swords to an arranged count, he lunged and I sank to earth gasping out my last heroic couplet.

My wooden sword worried me. It wouldn't convince the audience, would it? An intense lady took me aside. She had read everything from Kafka to Virginia Woolf, claimed intimacy with Augustus John and wore a boa in the style of Isadora Duncan. Through a haze of Balkan Sobranie she reminded me that this was no trivial Abbey kitchen comedy. This was poetic drama. Realism must not clip the wings of imagination.

The Persian was played by Alfred, a short-sighted, nervous man not destined for the stage. He spoke his lines without emphasis and teetered on the beer crates. His fatal lunge wafted harmlessly in the untroubled air. For the performance he wore a pleated tunic suitable for warriors Celtic, Egyptian, Roman or what-you-will. I was garbed likewise but carried a shield to identify my nationality.

Before curtain-up The Boa gave us advice. 'Release your emotions and let them flow.'

Alfred took her words to heart. With his entrance approaching I glanced into the wings. Sword at the ready, he was crouched on the beer crates like a giant frog ready to unleash himself, and before I had even reached his cue, he took off like Batman, cleaving right and left. Fortunately he was not wearing his glasses and aimed in the wrong direction, sailing past me to land on all fours. One glance at his frenzy and I decided to die like a dog and let the honour of Troy look after itself, but before I could dodge he was on his feet charging straight at me, sword pointed at my chest. I dived, but too late. The sword ripped through my tunic, sliced a weal across my ribs and sent me sprawling. My helmet flew like a cannonball into the wings, rebounded off the side wall and clattered like a lost hubcap into the audience. Winded, I gasped out my final couplet and gave up the ghost.

The curtain descended. We took our bow. Someone handed back

my helmet with a nasty grin. In the dressing room The Boa comment-
ed that if my death was not the noblest in the annals of Troy, it was
certainly the noisiest.

Ria Mooney left none of her students in doubt about the uncertainties of the stage. 'Because you give your life to the theatre,' she warned,
'don't presume that the theatre owes you a living in return.' For the
dedicated, her words were a challenge; for the rest, they were
sound advice to stick to the day job. Earning a living onstage was
precarious then – it is still no guaranteed bed of roses. Outlets were
few: there was little work on radio, advertising was almost unheard
of, films arrived from Hollywood once in a blue moon and television
had not yet been established. A young aspirant looked hopefully
towards the Abbey or the Gate, but the Abbey, with players under
permanent contract, offered few opportunities, the more so because
fluency in Irish was essential for membership of the company. The
Edwards/Mac Liammóir company and Longford Productions, who
shared the Gate, if not closed shops, cast from a limited pool of established players. After fruitless weeks in Dublin, actors young and old
looked towards the provinces for work.

I was six months or so in the Gaiety School when Ria took me
aside to tell me that Shela Ward, who ran a touring company, was
looking for an actor. If I was interested, she would suggest me. I could
have kissed her feet.

I purchased a basketwork skip and into it packed everything I
owned, a couple of suits, a sports jacket and slacks, a dinner suit,
pullovers, shirts, socks. I had been warned that on tour there was no
question of the company providing modern dress costumes. An actor

must provide his own, which had to include a dinner suit, for a minimum of seven plays. Working out how to dress differently for each play required planning, and it was an unwritten rule that an actor must not appear in public during the day wearing the outfit he would wear on stage that evening. Having a reasonably extensive personal wardrobe was part of the job, far removed from today's T-shirt and jeans, and the company provided the rest.

I lugged the skip to the quays and waited for the bus to Wexford, where I would join Equity Productions in the Theatre Royal. It was 1944. April the 1st. Make of that what you like. I've heard all the jokes.

A fit-up touring company, like its soul-mate the circus, was on the road hail, rain or snow, winter and summer, year in year out, breaking only for a week at Christmas and a few days at Easter. Monday was travelling day. After breakfast it was to the hall to load the hired lorry and move on. Journeys were short, sometimes no longer than ten or twelve miles to the nearest town. It was not yet the age of the automobile; an audience did not arrive by motor car from twenty or thirty miles distant, locals walked down the street to the parish hall.

Loading the lorry was not haphazard. Trunks and baskets were built into pillars at each corner. Scenery was laid flat on top and over the lot was thrown a tarpaulin to ward off rain and weather. Under the tarpaulin huddled the actors, like night-time in cardboard city, swathed in overcoats, rugs and what protection they could muster against the whistling wind.

The first job on arrival was to unload the truck and fit-up the stage. This is the origin of 'Fit-up', the generic term for touring companies where the actors not only did the acting but all the other work as well: loading and unloading the lorry, erecting the sets, collecting props and furniture, selling tickets at the box office and ushering the audience to their seats, as well as selling raffle tickets in the interval.

Touring companies rarely played in theatres. They played in 'The Hall' – the Parochial Hall, the Town Hall, the Confraternity Hall, Halla Naomh Gobnait, the Banba Ballroom or the Oisin, and, when cinemas were mushrooming in every town and village, importing not only the culture of Hollywood but fancier names for the local centres of entertainment, the company played in the Savoy, the Premier, the Astor and the De Luxe.

Halls were often so ill-equipped that it was out-and-about the town, borrowing porter barrels and planks to erect or extend the stage. Some halls were so cramped that the only way from one side of the stage to the other was to crawl under it, which revives a memory of coming face-to-face with Anna Manahan, she in a white evening dress, myself in a dinner suit, crawling on our hands and knees between abandoned scenery and spiders' webs under the stage in Abbeyfeale.

Every hall was the same: the caretaker nowhere in sight when the company arrived, the doors locked, kicking our heels until someone turned up with a key, lugging scenery up twisting stairs, floors unswept since the last *céilidh* and Old Time, dressing rooms smelling of stale beer and rattling with empties, the fuses blown, the front curtains discharging a dust storm when the tab line was pulled, the stage pelmet, all wolfhounds and round towers, hanging loose. Dressing rooms were make-do. In the Boathouse, so-called because it was one, the company dressed in a room at the back of the hall and reached the stage by a gangway outside the building that hung over a river. Tradition had it that on the night the Ghost of Hamlet's father failed to haunt Anew MacMaster, he had lost his footing and was splashing about in the River Blackwater.

More dramatic was what happened in a hall where the ceiling was so low that scenery could not be erected and curtains were hung around the stage to hide the bare walls. Squeezed between the curtains and the wall, an actor attempted a quick change of costume. Nose to the wall, he wriggled out of his trousers but when he raised his leg to pull on another pair, he wobbled, parting a join in the curtains that revealed his back to the audience. Which would have raised no more than a snigger had he not, in the cramped space, accidentally removed his underpants as well. The sight lasted no more than a few seconds but it left the audience stunned, and when the curtains closed again they remained riveted, wondering if they had imagined it and, at least the bawdier among them, hoping the apparition would reappear.

A company visited a town for a week and presented a different play each night. Something not too heavy for opening night that would send the audience home, happy and ready, to spread the word and encourage bigger audiences for the rest of the week. If the show was popular, the prospects for the week were good; if the punters left glum-faced a poor week was in store.

Finding an attraction to pull them in on Saturday night was a problem. Saturday night was for shopping, confession and the pub. As often as not, so few turned up at the box office that the company did not play. *Rebecca* by Daphne du Maurier was good for Saturday. It had that special appeal few plays have. *Peg O' My Heart* and *Charlie's Aunt* had it as well and, from the modern repertoire, so have *Sive*, *Dancing at Lughnasa* and *Big Maggie*. Whether it is the Abbey or the local dramatic society that presents them, star plays, like star actors, fill the house. When I was on tour, *Rebecca* was a star attraction and on Saturday nights it played to good houses when better plays languished before a dozen paying customers or did not play at all because so few turned up.

Professionals like to think that professionalism makes all the difference. It doesn't. National theatre or local dramatic society, if the punter enjoys the show, that's enough. Who worries about the architectural style if a house is warm and comfortable?

Sunday night was the big night. Turnstiles clicking, the hall packed to overflowing. Books of raffle tickets selling at tuppence each, or five for a tanner, the prize a quid or ten bob depending on a quick head-count of the audience. Members of the company sold the tickets. The rule was simple; those in straight make-up took the money at the door, showed the audience to their seats and sold the raffle tickets. Intellectuals, who thought a raffle undignified, got short shrift from the company manager, when the hall man and the lorry driver were paid out of a clinking bag of raffle money. Money was not always the prize. Naggins of whiskey were raffled. China teapots were raffled. An enterprising impresario with a finger on the pulse of the nation raffled statues and holy pictures, every one guaranteed to have been blessed in Lourdes. In later times some cowboy raffled an application form for an interview for the Radio Éireann Repertory Company.

Where to lay one's head for the week was a first concern. Hotels were out of the question – way beyond the pocket of a fit-up actor. On arrival in a town, the first port of call was the local lodging house, with its smells of Sunlight Soap and cabbage water. When there was no lodging house, or where the only one was occupied by permanent boarders – an unmarried schoolteacher, a surly fellow behind a newspaper who was an inspector of something-or-other, and a beery slob who was hail-fellow-well-met at night and gloomily truculent at breakfast – then it was knock on doors down back streets and bargain with housewives unaccustomed to catering, but anxious for a few extra shillings to make ends meet.

Nowadays, when I drive through Cahir I see the house where I lodged all those years ago. It was new then, county council-built. From the outside one suspected nothing of the poverty within. Four of the company required accommodation, two of the women and two of the men. Double rooms, of course, one for the ladies, one for the men. There was the usual haggling: did we require full board or to rent the rooms and have the use of the range? Rooms and use of the range, please. Which meant we would do our own cooking – rather the women of the company would do it – and the food would be better than anything put on the table by a part-time landlady.

Near the fireplace in Cahir was a wooden cradle, ornately carved, a labour of love. Beside it sat the man of the house. 'A lovely piece of work,' I said, expecting to be told he had fashioned it with his own hands or that it had come down through the family for four generations, but when he answered it was not to the cradle he pointed but at the infant in it. 'That, sir,' he said, 'is a Caesarean birth.'

I remember that cradle, the sleeping infant, the pride in the man's voice, as if the Caesarean birth of his child was his one distinction in a featureless life. It may well have been. His kitchen was sparsely furnished, a table, a few chairs, a stool, plates and cups, a kettle and pots. The floor was bare. Over the mantelpiece hung a religious picture. On the windowsill stood a mug of wildflowers. This was an all-too-familiar scene of life on the wrong side of town in the hungry years of the forties. But what surprised, what shocked, was that the room to be occupied by our ladies contained a bed and nothing more, and the room to be occupied by the men was entirely empty: no furniture; no curtains; no linoleum; nothing. A room as bare as it was on the day the young couple moved in. A deal was made and the sleeping problem solved by carrying the beds used in Robinson's *The Far-Off Hills* from the hall and erecting them in the men's bedroom and, on the night of the play, humping them to the hall for the show and back again to the digs afterwards.

This was my first close-up of how the other half of my comfortable world lived. On tour there was more to follow. In County Cork, the village of Glanworth was too small and too remote to boast a boarding house. From door to door the actors touted for a place to stay. I was delayed in the hall repairing a lighting fault, and it was tea time when word filtered through that a room was booked for me half a mile outside the village. If I couldn't get there until after the show, a candle would be burning in the window. I didn't like the sound of it, but it was that or sleep in the hall.

After the show I set off uphill along a lonely by-road. The night was black, the road deserted. Gone are the days when I buried my head under the blankets after reading Sheridan Le Fanu and shut my eyes when Dracula pushed back the coffin lid but, on that moonless night, when I could hardly see my hand in front of me, the farther away the lights of the village, the more firmly I clutched my Rosary beads. And I was doing fine until an unearthly groan from directly overhead made me take to my heels and keep running until I spied the sanctuary of a lit candle in a cottage window. Next morning on my way to the hall I would identify the high bank on top of which a cow had snorted, but the night was not yet over. I tapped on the cottage door but got no answer. I tapped again. Silence. Then it struck me that the door might be on the latch. I tried. It opened.

It is eerie to stand in a strange kitchen in the uncertain flickering of a candle. And to hear breathing, close by, low and regular. My hand shook when I raised the candle and held it aloft. In the soft light I could distinguish young children, two – or was it three? – in a cradle. Others were bedded near the last embers of the fire. All were asleep; all but one, who opened round eyes and stared at me in the unnervingly artless way of childhood, before dropping off to sleep again.

I had been told that my room was on the left. I tiptoed to it, opened the door and went inside. The room was tiny. In the front wall was a recessed window with a net half-curtain. An iron bed had on it a mattress and one blanket. It was a child's bed. I am over six feet tall, how was I to sleep? I wanted to run. But to where? The hall was locked and, moreover, I had no stomach for facing the moaning demon that had sent me scurrying half an hour before. Like it or lump it, here I was and I'd better make the best of it. I pulled my pyjamas over the woollen vest my mother insisted that I wear, 'You'll need it in the cold weather,' she had said. She was right, as mothers always are. I tucked my pyjamas into my socks and pulled a pullover over the lot. I laid my tweed overcoat over the single blanket and had a fellow-feeling for Johnny Forty Coats bedded in a freezing doorway. This was not home, with its soft mattress and hot water bottle, but fatigue is a powerful soporific and the moment I blew out the candle, almost resentfully, I dropped off and slept like a log.

Next morning it was wash and shave in a basin of cold water on the windowsill. This was long before it was thought essential to have a shower every day. The visible parts – hands, neck and face – were well scrubbed, the rest were treated to a bath on Saturday night, and for the rest of the week must look after themselves. On tour it was unwise to take for granted the comforts of a bathroom or an indoor lavatory.

One learned to choose between the newspaper-stuffed 'outside' or to hang on until one reached the hall where things might be better. In the forties 'hygiene' was a word new to my vocabulary. When I first heard of it I thought it was another American fad.

It is not because of the discomfort, or the trust of leaving a door on the latch for a stranger, that I remember Glanworth, but the young wife who was my landlady for a week. She had many children, steps of stairs from eight or nine years old to newborn twins, one of two sets, I was proudly told. Their home was a traditional cottage with a central kitchen and two bedrooms. It did not take me long to work out that, with one of the bedrooms given over to me, some of the family must sleep in the kitchen and the rest in the second bedroom, husband, wife and God knows how many children packed into a tiny room. With the passing days I got to know the young woman better than I would know her husband, who had already gone to work when I rose in the morning. The first time we met she addressed me as 'Sir', and I replied, as was the custom of the time, by calling her Mrs Whatever-her-name-was. She was young and full of life. She laughed when she told me how the brakes of her bicycle had failed when she'd sped downhill towards the village and went over the parapet of the bridge, bike and all, to land in the river and crawl out soaking but without a broken bone. Two months later one of the children was born – 'That lad over there, and not a thing wrong with him, thank God.' Her grit was what I admired, the brave face she turned to the unrelenting life from which she had no hope of escape. Or was it acceptance? Not supine giving in, but fighting the good fight to make the best of things, her act of faith in God, her anchor in a time when aspirations were as limited as luxuries. I was pleased, honoured too, when she dropped the 'Sir' and called me by my Christian name.

When I was leaving, I decided to offer her something more than the few shillings I was paying for the hire of the room. Lest I offend, I said something about buying a few sweets for the kids. She took the money and seemed grateful but there was an awkwardness in our parting. Walking down to the village for the last time I wondered if I had done the wrong thing by offering the extra couple of shillings. Of course not, her need was obvious, but what saddened me was that when she thanked me she did not use my Christian name but called me 'Sir'.

Before the days of theatrical agents an actor on the lookout for a job on tour kept an eye on the 'Stage' column of the *Irish Independent*. A typical ad would run *Wanted experienced actor for long tour. Best terms. Apply the X Players. This week Killaloe, next week Portroe.* Or *Wanted juvenile girl for leading roles. Turn preferred* – which meant that her talent for singing or juggling or doing the splits, in the variety show that followed the play, was more important than the young lady's acting ability.

If a company was unknown, or its credentials doubtful, there was always a risk in taking the job. Many an actor thumbed his way home when a cowboy management did a midnight flit, leaving the hall owner unpaid and the cast stranded. The other side of the coin was that a management suffered when, all unsuspecting, an actor was engaged who could neither memorise his lines nor control his thirst. One management, wearied by the human frailties of tippling old pros, included in their ads the warning that *Workshys and beer sharks need not apply.*

When an actor joined a touring company, there was no discussion about the roles he would play. His parts were those vacated by the actor he replaced. Be he young or old, were the part that of an Irish farmer or an English aristocrat, suitable or not, the vacant role was his and he must make shift as best he could. At the age of twenty, I was cast as a sixty-year-old and played the part wearing a ton of make-up, a railway junction of lake lines, a quavering voice and shaking hands. May God, and all those of sixty, forgive me.

If an actor cannot memorise, he is out of business. Two weeks was the usual rehearsal time allowed to a new arrival before he was on stage in the first of the plays. In that time he was expected to have learned as many as seven parts, some short, some long. Two weeks was generous. Many a gallant soul, if he had not been sent scripts in advance, was pitchforked onto the stage straight from the bus.

Youth absorbs lines like blotting paper, but the years take their toll. The long part, memorised in a couple of days at the age of twenty, takes infinitely longer when sixty comes and goes. Gone are the carefree days when I arrived at the hall for the evening performance and had to consult the show card at the entrance to discover which of the plays was billed for that night. Then it was don the costume and, at the rise of the curtain, press the appropriate memory button and off I'd go.

Actors have nightmares about forgetting lines, that glassy-eyed moment when memory fails and the words won't come. There is no more sickening experience on stage. My recurrent nightmare (I suffer from it still) is that I am in the wings, the play is in progress, and I don't know a word. Remorselessly my entrance approaches. I panic. I wake. I dare not fall asleep again lest the dream recurs.

Once I did not wake. I did not wake because I was not asleep. A company I joined postponed the opening of a new play planned for the following Sunday and replaced it with *Doctor Angelus* by James Bridie. It could be run up in a hurry, management said, because it had only recently been dropped from the rep and everyone knew the lines. Everyone, except me, of course. I'd have a bit of learning to do but I was a quick study, wasn't I? A crisis was a crisis, the company depended on me, the show must go on and all that jazz.

I was to play the Doctor but what I did not realise until the script was in my hand was that the action revolved around Angelus and his assistant, Johnston, and that both parts were a mile long. Don't worry, I was told, Jack has played Johnston and he'll keep things going if you get into trouble. How was I to know that Jack had swallowed the same sob story and agreed to play Johnston because he believed that I had played Angelus? At our first rehearsal the truth dawned, but not for a moment did it strike either of us to protest. We had a couple of days, hadn't we? The company relied on us. Actors gotta do what actors gotta do.

The scripts never left our hands. They were propped against milk jugs. They were ringed by pint glasses. We topped-up on black coffee and slogged into the small hours, but we never had a chance. When curtain-up arrived, we knew the first act and had what is known as 'a working knowledge' of the second. The third act was largely unmapped territory, leaving us to do what many a gallant thespian had done before us – keep to the story line and gag our way through.

'To gag' means to have a cool head when a line is missed, to think fast and come up with something that will keep the play moving until someone gets it back on script. Nowadays, with adequate rehearsal periods, actors have ample time to memorise and the hissing of the prompter is no longer a feature of opening nights. But when plays went on stage after only a week's rehearsal and actors played on the completed set for the first time on the first night, wearing costumes and handling props seen for the first time at that afternoon's dress rehearsal, even the most diligent player was in danger of missing a line, and panicky prompters behind the fireplace chain-smoked through a packet of twenty.

Whole scenes, whole plays, have been improvised. An actor of a generation before me, Bert Lena, regaled me with tales of a summer season when he played sixty different plays on sixty successive nights of a summer season. This was no miracle of memory but the skill of improvisation. In the morning the company gathered and agreed the story line of the night's play. Each was allotted his part – the lover, the parent, the faithful wife, the vile seducer and so on. Then it was home for boiled beef and semolina pudding and back for the evening performance.

Unfortunately, neither Jack nor I was a master of improvisation; we depended on a script. Long speeches were little trouble: memorise the sequence, keep the overall plot in mind, and make it up as you go along. After one long speech I threw in a bit of dramatics, got a round of applause, and wondered how that would go down in Ria Mooney's school of acting.

Dialogue was the problem, it required knowing the lines and giving cues. Jack and I got through the first act well enough and kept the second act staggering along, aided by those sufficiently versed in the text to speak not only their own lines but some of ours as well. But when the curtain came down for the second interval we were showing the scars of battle. Jack sat staring into space. When he was called for the third act he dragged himself to the stage like a fated Mallory on the slopes of Everest. A charge of adrenaline would come to his rescue, I thought, but his supply was exhausted.

The act opened with Jack on stage and me entering with a breezy 'Good morning, Doctor Johnston.'

No answer.

I tried again. 'Good morning, Doctor Johnston.'

Silence. Deep, resentful silence. The silence of one who understands, too late, that he has been led like a lamb to the slaughter.

Once more I tried. 'Good morning, Doctor.'

A bloodshot eye was turned on me. Viciously Jack hissed, 'Get on with it yourself. I'm fucked.' That was it. He'd opted out. Single-handed, I must sail the ship into harbour.

I would like to record a storybook ending that I got a standing ovation and half-a-dozen curtain calls for dedication above and beyond the call of duty, but real life isn't like that. The act stumbled on through hesitations and anguished silences. It was all downhill with no brakes and a stone wall at the bottom. At last, like a mercy killing, the curtain fell. In the dressing room someone said 'Well done.' My answer was two brief, blistering words.

Jack and I had sacrificed ourselves to the great theatrical tradition that, storm or tempest, death or destruction, *the show must go on*. Actors are no less vulnerable to illness or calamity than anyone else, but few professions have an absentee rate lower than that of the theatre. Actors regularly go onstage where in other jobs an ailment would be sufficient for a doctor's cert and a week off to recuperate. Only major theatre companies have regular understudies yet, night after night, all over the world, thousands of performances are staged and rarely is one cancelled. Actors have performed with a doctor on standby in the wings. Maureen Toal, long before she became a star of *Glenroe*, played propped in a chair, her foot in plaster, because earlier in the day she had sprained her ankle. On tour I helped to carry the stretcher bearing a player suffering from pleurisy to the hall before the show and home again afterwards. Anna Manahan went onstage in Egypt a few hours after the tragic, sudden death of her husband, Colm. So too did Donna Dent, on the evening of her mother's death, during the run of a Christmas show in the Gate. No less dedicated was the actress who gave a rattling good performance in the full knowledge that the Fraud Squad was waiting in the wings to interview her. And what of the impresario, Noel Pearson, when the proscenium arch of the Olympia collapsed on opening day? With astounding resourcefulness he moved the show, lock, stock and barrel to the Stella in Phibsborough, where the curtain went up on time. That's showbiz.

Actors have considerable pride in their work. Not that there is anything exclusive about the theatrical profession. I do not doubt that the same glow of satisfaction is known to the businessman when he is responsible for a firm's success, to the PR man when his client makes the front page, and to the paparazzi when his telephoto lens catches the international personality in an unguarded moment of topless abandon.

Touring actors were on the outskirts of society. They were 'the play crowd', 'the circus', persons of no fixed abode, beyond the pale of suburbia and the province of strong farming, the one no less conservative than the other. Small towns, and indeed large towns, closely observed the movements of a visiting company: 'The stringy fella with the long overcoat, he wouldn't be a Protestant, would he? He's staying with Maggie Doyle and she tells me he doesn't bless himself before meals. And the blondie fella – is the hair dyed, is it? He was here with a show last year singing and dancing wearing a woman's dress. Is he all right, is he? The walk of him you'd wonder. And tell us, would you be engaged to the good-looking one in the slacks, and the two of you staying with Mrs Finnerty? And with your father a postmaster, isn't it a wonder you're not in a cushy job in the civil service.' And, inevitably, the vital question, 'You'll want to know the time of mass on Sunday?'

In Michelstown, one of our company – the above-mentioned 'good looking one in the slacks' – was staying in the same digs as myself. She was a Protestant and on Sunday morning enquired about the time of service in the Protestant church. Our landlady was non-plussed. She did not know the time of service. She did not even know the location of the Protestant church. Jokingly, I said, 'You'd better come to mass with me.' 'Do, girl,' said our landlady. 'it will do you more good than the other place.'

On stage or off, strong language was taboo. At home, in school, in the billiards hall, in the pub or on the football field, woe to him who used the four-letter word. He could expect at least a reprimand, at worst a request to leave. Parents disapproved, so did teachers, referees, publicans and the caretaker of the CYMS. What was frowned on off stage was not acceptable on it.

As with modesty of language, so with modesty of dress: a nude scene would have been unthinkable. No management would have suggested it; no player would have agreed to it; no audience would have tolerated it. Forty years on I toured with a thriller in which the victim, a young woman, was undressed before being carried off stage. The only reaction I recall was in a West Cork town where a lady in the best seats whispered to her daughter, 'Your father will be sorry now that he didn't come.'

The first play in Dublin I can remember that included a nude scene was *Equus*. Maria McDermottroe, who played the scene, told me that on the first night she was terrified of what might happen:

protests out front; letters to the papers; her name dragged in the mud. In the event, if there were objections, they were muted. A southern company later toured the play and, in fear of possible objections, dimmed the lights to a minimum during the nude scene. That was the box office trying to have it both ways. Why did they not, as other companies did, play the scene without the actors undressing? Keeping the gear on does not make a prude. Shedding it does not make a liberal.

Touring quickly educated me in the ways of the world. I discovered that an actress on whom I had cast an eye was more than just a 'friend' of the older lady who lodged with her. The company made no comment, and most were strict Catholics.

And there was Billy, high-spirited and entertaining. When plans to introduce a new play into the rep were delayed because we were short of an actress to play the maid, Billy volunteered to take it on, and Annie D'Alton – we were with her company at the time – was happy to let him have a go.

At rehearsal Billy did not put a foot wrong, and on the first night, in cap and apron, subtly made-up and discreetly convincing above the waist, he would have fooled anyone. His first scene went well. The audience did not notice a thing. His next appearance was with a tray. He clattered cups. He took all night to lay the table. Still the audience did not guess. Next time, his walk was slinky, his eye roving. When someone out front giggled, that was the end of it. He batted his eyelids. The back rows sniggered and serious characterisation sank without a trace.

In variety Billy was in his element. He enjoyed his song and dance act far more than acting, and on a night when he did not change out of costume after the show, I was with him when he sauntered down the main street of Ballybay, County Monaghan, wearing a full-length green evening dress and silver high-heeled shoes. Heads turned. Conversations broke off in mid-sentence. A hall door opened and a woman in disbelief called over her shoulder to two or three others, who joined her, mouths agape like nestlings awaiting the mother bird.

We were lodging in a pub, and it was after closing time when we got there. The bar was in semi-darkness. After-hours drinkers huddled in a corner. When Billy made his entrance there were mutterings about the quare fella in the woman's frock. Billy revelled in it. He planked himself at the drinker's table and called on the landlord to 'bring down the box' and, after-hours or not, the Sergeant on the prowl or not, he led a sing-song into the small hours, camping it up but never going so far that he could not turn the first hint of hostility into a laugh.

In a time when homosexuality earned violent condemnation, how did he get away with it? Brazenness? Because he made them laugh? Because he was one of the 'play crowd' and would be gone on Monday morning? Because, above all, he was a man of warmth and irresistible high spirits, or was it because those present knew more than they pretended, because nod and wink and look the other way was common practice? Nevertheless, under the boisterousness, I sensed a jagged edge. A wrong step by Billy and I might hear again what I once heard in another place, 'He'd better mind himself. The lads went after a nancy-boy once and he didn't do it again because he'd nothing to do it with.' It was not from a half-drunk moralist urinating into a ditch, behind a mountain shebeen, that I heard those words but from a gowned academic in a university common room.

The theatre took a more liberal view. Even in those not-so-far-back days, when so much that would later emerge was covered up and denied, when the truth about abortion, infanticide, physical abuse and paedophilia was hidden so successfully that many were genuinely unaware of the unhealthy underbelly of our respectable society, even then, the theatre had little sympathy for prejudice or racism. In the theatre, no one bothered if a performer was gay, no one worried if the director was a woman, no one questioned the colour of an actor's face. Talent counted, not pigmentation or sexual inclination.

In my early days, a touring repertoire of Abbey successes was the usual bill. Sean O'Casey, Lennox Robinson, Paul Vincent Carroll, Louis D'Alton and George Shiels were stock-in-trade. Ireland was still a largely agricultural, non-industrial society. Every second person in the city had ties with farming cousins or the hometown family shop. Matchmaking, squabbling about wills and the double-dealing of gombeen men were common themes. An occasional thriller varied the bill as did, inevitably, a romantic comedy. *Peg O' My Heart* was an enduring favourite, a rags-to-riches story of an impish Irish girl winning her way into the hearts of an upper-class family and a final-curtain engagement to her wealthy hero. Like many another popular piece of writing of the time, *Peg* came from a literary stable that presented Irish characters as quaintly comic. Their appeal was not only to English and American audiences but to an Irish society still familiar with the old Ascendancy. Writers superior to J. Hartley Manners, the author of *Peg*, had long been masters of the device – Lever, Lover, Boucicault, Somerville and Ross, and M. J. Farrell spring to mind – but it must be emphasised that they presented an authentic picture of the social structure of their time and, if they patronised, it was with affection not malice. And who in a native Irish audience did not enjoy the blarney of an Irish servant talking rings round his bemused big house master?

Two of the plays in the rep of my first company, Equity Productions, were far from bland. *Things That Are Caesar's* by Paul Vincent Carroll, and *Thy Dear Father* by Gerard Healy, were severely critical of contemporary attitudes. It would be gratifying to claim that their inclusion in the rep was part of a liberal agenda (the term had not yet been invented), but the truth was that they were toured because they were Abbey successes and were expected to attract an audience.

The central character in *Things That Are Caesar's* is a young woman forced into an arranged match condoned by the parish priest. She is no shrinking Sive, and in defiance of the parish priest she walks out on her husband and her Irish doll's house. The second play, *Thy Dear Father*, traces the mental breakdown of a son goaded towards the priesthood by a sanctimonious mother, a woman typical of Roman Catholic motherhood, whose fondest dream was to see her son ordained into the priesthood. That these plays could be toured without protest casts an interesting light on a time that was Church-dominated and intellectually repressive. An explanation may be that rural Ireland was only too familiar with the arranged match and the craw-thumping mother buying her way into Heaven with a priest in the family. But, while accepting such plays, a distinction was drawn between an attack on the Catholic faith and the criticism of an authoritarian parish priest or a sanctimonious mother. Had the plays criticised Catholic beliefs, they would not have gone far without walk-outs and protests.

These were times devoutly faithful to Roman Catholicism, when few were prepared to challenge the all-powerful parish priest for whom control of local society, particularly its education, was essential if Church authority was to be maintained. Paul Vincent Carroll's criticism was not of the Catholic faith but of the misuse of priestly power. He addressed a society that, as he saw it, wore a muzzle without protest. The intellectual argument in his plays *Shadow and Substance* and *The White Steed*, as in *Things That Are Caesar's*, is between priest and schoolmaster, accepted at the time to be two of the three best-educated members of a small community. The third was the local doctor, usually presented as wise, avuncular, on call night, noon and morning, slow to request a fee and dedicated to the society in which he worked.

A favourite character of Carroll's was the independent-minded girl. He used her to telling effect in *Things That Are Caesar's* and *The White Steed*. She was a first cousin of Nora in Ibsen's *A Doll's House* and H. G. Wells's *Ann Veronica*. She was a forerunner of the admirable race of young women, so different from the dimpled maidens of my youth, who year by year fight for equality in a fiercely protected man's world. Carroll's heroine dared where men hesitated: she walked out on her marriage, she defied the priest. Meeting her in *Things That Are Caesar's* was a revelation. Prior to that I could not have believed that any girl, any 'respectable' girl, would act with such defiance and irresponsibility. But as I came to understand the play, I came to understand that to defy a priest was not to defy the Church and that one can think independently without wishing to subvert society.

Despite antipathy to Carroll's writing in certain clerical centres, I remember no objections when *Things That Are Caesar's* was played in halls run by the local parish priest, which many halls were. At the time, priests were barred from attending the theatre, a peculiar rule for those enjoined to supervise the faith and morals of their flocks. The result was that, in the days of the bicycle clip, the Abbey and plays of ideas were worlds apart from rural Ireland. Another result was to trip over many a more enlightened priest watching from the wings during a performance.

Nostalgia paints a picture of touring companies playing night after night to enthusiastic full houses hungry for drama. Not so. I was touring with Annie D'Alton and John Cowley when hard times hit. The hall was less than half-full on the first night and three-quarters empty on the second. On the third night I was on box office duty and, with no customers to keep me occupied, I lounged on the hall steps looking down an empty street. Not a dog barked, not a soul was in sight, not a corner boy supported a wall, not a couple of ould ones gossiped at a pump. For five minutes nothing moved. Then from the end of the street came the unoiled screeching of an ancient bicycle. It was ridden by a skeleton in a gabardine raincoat, a peaked cap over his eyes. Along the street he came, peering right and left, a lost soul in search of diversion. Passing the hall he spotted the billboard advertising our plays, and came to a stop with a foot dragging on the ground in lieu of brakes. Critically, he scanned the list of plays. Just as critically he scanned me. 'How much is it in?'

'Two and six – one and six and a shilling.'

'Be God, you'll be a long time getting two and a kick out of me. Is it a show?'

'It's a play.'

'What's it called?'

'*Things That Are Caesar's*.'

'What's it about?'

'It's about a girl who walks out on her marriage.'

'Be Jay, that's a quare class of a thing to have a play about.'

Down the street he gazed, and up the street. He lit a butt. He fished in his pocket and extracted, coin by coin, a sixpence, a threepenny bit and three pennies. 'I'll give it a try. It better be good.'

In the interval, when I was selling raffle tickets, I found him warming his backside on a tepid radiator at the back of the hall. For two minutes he deliberated between two for a penny or five for tuppence. At last he made up his mind. 'I'll chance a deuce. When does the singing start?'

'What singing?'

'The singing and dancing.'

'This is a play.'

'I thought the play was over. You mean there's more?'

'Two acts more.'

'And no singing? Jaysus, give me back me deuce. I don't know will I bother to stay."

He didn't. And more like him. Which was the cue for the management to take action: if variety was what they wanted, variety was what they'd get.

It was common for touring companies to offer a night's entertainment of 'Drama, Variety and Laughable Farce' – a play, followed by song and dance, followed by comic knockabout. This was an echo from Victorian theatre, when the evening commenced with a one-act play to occupy the groundlings until the carriage trade arrived for the main attraction and was rounded off with an interlude of song and dance to revive the flagging libido of wearied Empire-builders.

Annie D'Alton ran a drama-only company, one of the best on the road, but needs must when the devil drives. The hall piano was dusted off and anyone with a turn to offer, song, skit or recitation, was ordered to brush it up. Billy Quinn and Sonny Coll did a double act, someone told a few jokes and a sketch was thrown in for good measure. Pauline Flanagan offered 'The Trimmings on the Rosary', a popular recitation when the family Rosary was embedded in Irish life.

The homely verses tugged at the heart strings, recalling the nightly Rosary with the family bowed in prayer, chairs for pews, backsides in the air, the man of the house leading the first decade, his missus the next, and, following them, the children. And if Aunt Nellie, whose husband died last year, God rest him, had come to visit, her decade was not forgotten. Following the Rosary came the Trimmings, an affectionate name for the prayers tagged on for special personal or family or intentions, for Mick who had emigrated to the States, for fine weather for the harvest, a Hail Mary for the Foreign Missions and a Glory Be for the grace of a happy death.

Popular ballads rarely pass the test of literary excellence but they are matchless expressions of popular sentiment. 'The Trimmings on the Rosary' drew a reassuring picture of close-knit Irish family life cemented by religious faith, and when Pauline had finished the last line she won rounds of applause as heartfelt as any she would earn as a distinguished performer with the Abbey or under Joe Dowling's direction in Minneapolis.

After that tour with Annie D'Alton, Pauline and I did not meet until I was playing in the Lyric in Belfast and she arrived to rehearse for *Juno and the Paycock*. 'Is it forty or forty-five years since we played together?' was our jaunty greeting. That is the way of the theatre: actors work together for a few years, take off in different directions, then meet again after a lifetime and pick up the friendship exactly where it left off. I worked with Pauline for the last time in *Tarry Flynn* in the Abbey. When she and her husband George visited Ireland we always had a most enjoyable lunch date in the Arts Club. She died not long after the death of my wife Nancy. I remember her as a fine actress and a warm, affectionate friend.

Our leading man was John Cowley, who would become a

household name in *The Riordans*. His variety act was so far off the beaten track that I was taken completely by surprise. It was a boxing commentary, a recreation of the famous heavyweight bout between Joe Louis, the American champion, and the German Max Schmeling. I expected a comic turn, or an impersonation of some well-known sports commentator of the day, a Michael O'Hehir or a Raymond Glendenning. I could not believe that John would simply retell the story of a fight so well-known that everyone, not just boxing enthusiasts, knew it blow by blow. But that's what he did. Sitting on a chair on an empty stage, without the aid of background crowd effects, he built up the excitement of the fight from the cautious sparring of the opening rounds to the fury of the knockout. His audience was with him from the first bell, and he was cheered to the echo when the knock-out blow was delivered. It was as if those out front were listening to a live commentary. Which in a way they were. The fifties had no television channel covering every sport, from wall-to-wall football to the erotic delights of synchronised swimming. Nor had everyone a radio. When a big match was on the air, the house that boasted a wireless propped the set on the windowsill for the street to gather and listen in. Running commentaries were few and far between. Enthusiasts sat on a roadside gate to have the result of a match shouted from a car on the way home from the game, or waited until the next day to read a newspaper report of the match, two half-columns and a photograph were about what a big game was worth. In those times winning or losing was not a national issue. Sport was an optional extra, not one of life's priorities.

Were audiences more naïve two generations back? Of course not. Granted that, in days of melodrama, warnings were shouted from the audience when the designing Sir Jasper stalked the virtuous heroine.

But, in recent times, how many blessed themselves when the Bishop finished his sermon in *The Field*? And if 'Cheer the hero, hiss the villain' is pantomime stuff, which of us did not want to cheer when the bicycles took off in *E.T.*? Viewers know that a soap is no more than television entertainment, but for some it becomes a kind of parallel reality, a fusion of pseudo-life with the real thing. The experience is akin to that of acting. An actor immerses himself in the fictional character he is playing while a part of him stands aside, observing and controlling the technique of his performance. He does not 'live the part', he 'acts'. If he lived the part of a murderer, there would be a dead body on stage every night and the imagination cartwheels at the prospect of playing Don Juan.

A young actor, expecting a bit of a laugh, once questioned me about the standard of fit-up companies. A fair question, and to answer it I explained that touring theatre must be measured against the standards of its own time, not of ours. Some companies were very poor indeed, but the leading companies were training grounds for many actors who would later make names for themselves in the Dublin theatre and further afield. Lest my young friend doubt me, I named some of the players who were members of the first company I joined, Equity Productions: Anna Manahan did her groundwork with the company, Eddie and Geoff Golden, both of whom later joined the Abbey, worked with it, as did Maura Deady who played Mrs Riordan in *The Riordans*, and her husband Johnny Hoey played Francie in the same soap. Seamus Breathnach would later become head of drama in Radio Éireann, and Shela Ward, a founder of the company, had spent a number of years in the Abbey before taking to the road. A strong cast by any reckoning.

Annie D'Alton was first on stage; she was carried on as a child, and she had proudly notched up nearly sixty years on the boards when I got to know her. She was a vivacious performer, in her fifties and still playing Peg in *Peg O' My Heart* and Tomasina, the scatter-brained Canon's niece, in *Shadow and Substance*.

Audiences loved Annie. She never missed a laugh, which I learned to my cost when playing Alaric to her Peg. I cut across one of her lines and got a dagger look onstage and a lecture in the dressing room for stepping on one of her laughs. 'Timing, dear,' she explained; 'it's all about timing.' She was right, all comedy is about timing.

She was far from laughter when she, John Cowley and myself were sitting in a gloomy digs on a gloomy afternoon, staring into a gloomy fire that offered no defence against the winter cold. The performance of *Juno and the Paycock*, due on stage that evening, was in trouble. The cast was short by two actors, discarded in the town we had left that morning. Drink was the trouble, and a landlady clamouring for her rent before the Monday morning lorry carried the guilty pair beyond her reach. Twice previously it had occurred and twice Annie had bailed them out. Twice was enough. 'Don't pay them until last thing on Sunday night after the show,' she instructed me – I was her business manager – 'that will keep them out of harm's way.'

It did not. For the third time they arrived at the lorry on Monday morning, hung-over and flat broke. Annie had had enough: they had let down her good name; they had let down the company; they had let down the profession. 'Leave them behind,' she ordered. I did not think she meant it but she did, and the lorry, with the company on board, pulled away, leaving two unbelieving faces staring after it. A stern lesson for the culprits, but a problem for the rest of the company faced with playing *Juno* that evening with a cast short by two. Such things have been done. Theatre legend retailed how a cowboy manager played both Maningham, the villain, and Rough, the detective, in the same performance of *Gaslight*, even arresting himself at the final curtain. But *Juno* was not *Gaslight*. *Juno* was sacred text, and none could feel happy at the prospect of Bentham skipping offstage to return thirty seconds later as Needle Nugent, or Joxer donning a slouch hat and trench coat to reappear as the Mobiliser.

More than that, Annie's stomach was 'closed', a physical condition, peculiar to her, that was induced by company difficulties. When it struck, Annie sat wrapped in rugs, looking pained, waited-on with eggnogs and port wine by Sonny Coll, actor, song and dance man, and comforter of the afflicted. On the day we abandoned the actors, the attack of closed stomach was severe. Into this dejection entered the McFaddens. They were passing through, they said, and hearing that Annie was in town had dropped in to say hello. Annie was in no form for socialising. She listened glumly while the McFaddens shop-talked about how they had abandoned the fit-ups for mobile cinema. Behind their chatter was a note of regret. 'Cinema,' they said, 'is not the same as proper touring, is it? You're lucky, Annie, to have real people around you.' Annie glared. Two of her company were missing and her stomach was closed. Bitterly, she answered, 'It's all right for you, you can keep the buggers in a box.'

Annie was a tough battler. 'I'll die on the barricades,' she declared, and if fortune dealt her a good hand towards the end of her career when she played Minnie in *The Riordans*, it was no more than she had earned.

For the record, the missing actors turned up, leg-weary and mud-spattered, having walked the twelve miles from the previous town. *Juno* went on with a full cast and future landladies were paid on time, as far as I know.

Touring was a potential trap. It tempted actors to drift from town to town acting by numbers, with no incentive to try harder. I remember Noel D'Alton, brother of the playwright Louis D'Alton, spent his life on the road. He was an actor of considerable talent. 'Why don't you try your luck in Dublin or London?' I asked him. 'In the winter when it's cold I think about it,' he said. 'Then it's spring and I ramble out the road and sit in the sun, and ask myself, "What's wrong with this?"'

I had no wish to spend a lifetime on the road. When I was starting, the fit-ups were an adventure, but it was time to move on. I had seen my share of worn faces and the disenchantment of ageing actors huddled over niggardly fires in comfortless digs, with nowhere to go after a lifetime on the road but the charity of a spare room in the home of a married sister, their epitaph a dressing-room exchange between two senior players: 'Where's old Johnny now? I haven't heard of him for years.' 'Dead, I suppose, the poor old devil.'

And the caravan travels on.

3

Tours come, tours go. They are part of the actor's game. I met Stanley Illsley and Leo McCabe, of IMP Productions, on a tour of Northern Ireland in the late forties. It was run under the banner of CEMA, The Committee for the Encouragement of Music and the Arts, a title redolent of high-mindedness and the Tory work ethic.

Stanley Illsley was all neurotic energy. An English leading man once described him as the only person he knew who moved in three directions simultaneously. On the rehearsal floor he danced jigs of exasperation when things did not go his way. His tantrums caused strong actors to quail and sensitive actresses to shed tears. Not Leo, the businessman of the partnership. He moved with the gravity of an ocean liner in a fog, impervious to Stanley's frenzies. When he was slow on lines, Stanley's clicking fingers upset everyone but him. If he delayed a curtain because he was finishing a cigarette – I was present when it happened – he came onstage only when he was ready, unruffled by Stanley's cry of 'Make way for Sir Henry Bloody Irvine.'

Getting away with a tantrum depends on who you are. In the big bad world of film, a star can terrorise the rehearsal floor with a tantrum, or delay the cameras while he, or she, sleeps it off. Stars are tolerated because they make the box office jingle; lesser fry are sacked.

Milo O'Shea, Daphne Carroll and Doreen Keogh were members of the company. The plays were Goldsmith's *She Stoops to Conquer*, in which I played A Servant, a light comedy, *George and Margaret*, in which I had a lot of fun as Dudley, the high-spirited son, and *Juno and the Paycock* once again. This time I played the Mobiliser. In Newry, my exit line at the end of Act Two, 'Boyle, no man can do enough for Ireland,' won a round of applause. In Portadown, the curtain descended in wintry silence.

Leo McCabe was a competent actor, if never one to stir an audience. Stanley's undoubted talent was too often dissipated by overacting, particularly in comedy. He directed himself and lacked the control of a guiding hand. When he played the photographer in J. B. Priestley's *When We Are Married*, it was not enough that his tripod caught in the lintel of the door, it must catch three times and he must trip as well. Playing Thomas More in the Olympia, he paused for so long on each step up to the scaffold that an anxious voice in the audience wondered if More would meet his Maker in time for the last bus.

Stanley was a kind man. It hurt me when others caricatured his overacting. Some years later, working with him in a television play, even though he was at sea in the world of cameras, it was a pleasure to see how well he acted under the discipline of a good director.

My only real memory of that tour was that on it I celebrated my twenty-first birthday. Cigarettes rained in boxes of twenty, from members of the company, and Stanley and Leo invited me to dinner. It was the first of many birthdays I would spend away from home. I did not announce it – a phone call from my parents broke the word. The fuss of celebration embarrasses me. I wonder what is special about a chance date on a calendar, yet on birthdays away from home I feel solitary and often lonely. I wait in hope for the phone to ring. If it does, I play down the anniversary, if it does not I hope it will.

I once astonished my children by telling them that during my time in Dublin I stayed in twenty-eight different digs, lodging houses and so-called flats, in some for a couple of weeks, in some for a few months, depending on the unpredictability of my itinerant profession.

On Rathgar Road I still pass a tall house near the church where I lodged for a few months. I remember it for the farcical mini-drama in which I was the leading, and only, performer. To set the scene, I was the odd man out among the 'paying guests', who were civil servants and other diligent members of the community, long-gone to honest toil before I faced the day, and the disapproval of a landlady who thought it immoral not to hold down a nine-to-five permanent and pensionable job. My time to leave was eleven, hair Brylcreemed, shoes polished, ready to parade down the front path like one without a care in the world and a chequebook to prove it. Out of sight of the base-ment kitchen I counted my pennies and waited for the tram.

Roberts Café in Grafton Street was the place to shop-talk and tap the grapevine for news of work. In the afternoon it was to the cinema, killing time. Actors have a lot of time to kill: waiting around between scenes at rehearsal, waiting all day for the evening performance, and that most trying time of all, waiting for the next job.

Almost in mockery of my impecunious state, a bag of golf clubs had been added to my worldly goods. The idea was my father's. The bag was huge. He had bought it after a trip to the Irish Open Championship in Portmarnock to see Henry Cotton play but, unlike the great golfer, he had no caddy to lug it around eighteen holes and it was passed on to me. I had played golf since I was a boy and missed the game when I was on tour. Now that I had hopes of digging-in in Dublin, I dreamed of rolling fairways and lengthy drives down the middle, but with no work in sight, I must practise putting on the bedroom linoleum while the golf bag sulked in a corner.

Work was slow to come. My belt was tightened. The tram ride to the city became a walk. Attending the cinema went by the board. I bird-watched the ducks in Stephen's Green. I sheltered from the rain in the National Gallery and suffered depression in the ponderous silence of the National Museum.

Before Christmas the tide turned. I was engaged, again by Illsley/McCabe, for a four-week season in Cork, to be followed by four weeks in the Olympia. Good news, but rehearsal would not commence until January and I must go home for Christmas. Only duty or calamity was an acceptable excuse for not going home for Christmas, and I was hard-up. I could manage the train fare, but how was I to buy presents and put on a bit of a show? I was no longer a permanently broke university student. I had made my run for fame and fortune and sardonic eyes would measure my success or failure by my readiness to buy a round.

There was only one way out – the three brass balls of the pawnbroker's shop, known to students as Uncle Joe's. In university days the pawnshop was a source of beer money until the registered letter arrived from home, or for a diverting eavesdrop on an exchange that might have come from an O'Dea/O'Donovan pantomime – 'Not the Little Flower again, missus.'

'Honest to God, Joe, a jewboy who sells holy pictures said the frame alone is worth a quid.'

'Well you can tell him from me, missus, that I have enough Little Flowers and Saint Anthonys and Pontius Pilates washing their hands to sanctify Maynooth itself. Two bob, missus. Take it or leave it.'

I did not pawn haphazardly. I decided not to pledge one item for a large sum, but a number of large items for small sums, making them easier to recover when my ship came home. The nearest pawnshop was in Richmond Street, close to the Grand Canal. Two suits and a jacket went over the counter, an evening suit went with them, all neat and tidy in a leather suitcase and, after some debate, my golf bag and set of clubs. With good husbandry, all would be redeemed within a couple of months when I started work.

Once more in funds, I headed home to Youghal, for by now my father had retired and purchased a bungalow there. Christmas came and went. I flashed a few quid and was back in Dublin ready for rehearsal. I took to the tram again. I viewed the world benignly from a front seat on the top deck and basked in the promise of a rosy future. On a morning when the sky was cloudless I clanked languidly into Rathmines. The green dome of the Church was washed in sunlight, the round face to the Town Hall clock was an orb of contentment. From the top deck I could see all the way down to Portobello and the tall houses of Richmond Street. In the sky there was smoke. On Portobello Bridge a crowd was gathering.

My blood went cold. The pawnshop – my pawnshop – was on fire! Flames belched from the windows, smoke billowed through holes in the roof. The fire brigade swarmed like water beetles. All that was missing was a distraught damsel shrieking in a top window, and a gallant fireman climbing to her rescue, the heroic moment to be immortalised by a front-page photograph in the *Evening Mail*.

When the flames died down, only the shell of the upper floors stood over the blackened remains of the downstairs shop. My wardrobe was gone, and with it my dreams of golfing afternoons and marble cake on a sunlit club veranda.

A few days after the fire, a notice went up on the charred front door to say that certain items had been saved. I hadn't a hope, but I called just in case. Ahead of me stretched a motley crew clutching pawn tickets. Behind a counter Uncle Joe compared tickets with numbers in a ledger – 'Sorry, mam. Lost in the fire. Sorry.'

'What good is sorry? Jemmy has no suit to wear on Sunday. The way he's carrying on, you'd think 'twas me burned the place down.'

I handed in my ticket. Uncle Joe consulted his ledger, turned a dozen pages, and consulted again. Next, he faced the ledger towards me, 'Look at that, son, a list of items in the room where your stuff was stored. Every item has a line drawn through it, meaning it was burned, except two. A suitcase and a bag of golf clubs. You're steeped, son. Steeped. You must have paid a fortune to St Anthony.'

I staggered up Rathmines Road under the weight of the suitcase and the bag of golf clubs. At the church I sat in the back row and took a breather. I put half-a-dollar in the poor box, and promised another seven-and-six to Saint Anthony when I could afford it. He is a forgiving saint. He must be owed a fortune.

I first heard of Anew McMaster on the way to school, when my father pointed to a yellow poster in a shop window. Puzzled, he said, 'A new

McMaster, how could that be? Surely no one is pretending to be a new McMaster? We all know who he is.' I didn't, not even when my father solved the mystery by spotting that the capital A had been separated in the printing from the 'new' of McMaster's first name, Anew. It was the 1930s. The first talking picture had just been shown in the local cinema, and infant wireless crackled in the headphones of radio enthusiasts. The travelling show was a feature of small-town life. Small groups, often no more than extended families, with actors doubling and often tripling the small parts, presented melodramas and tear-jerkers, potted versions of *The Colleen Bawn*, and anything and everything with a good box-office name. Travelling from crossroads to crossroads, playing to small audiences under canvas, leaky slates or galvanised iron, paying royalties was not for the small companies. One group presented a shorthand version of *The Informer* and, so the story runs, when Liam O'Flaherty turned up to see a performance of it somewhere in the West, their breath gagged and their hearts stopped beating. But the great man was benign. He shook hands, wished the company well and, smiling, went on his way. Relieved, the caravan rolled on, and, true to the best advertising instincts of showbiz, proudly announced in future venues that the author had seen and praised the performance.

Of all the companies on the road, that of Anew McMaster was the best known and most respected. Annually, with his company, Mac, as he was affectionately known, toured the towns of Ireland, large and small, presenting a repertoire of Shakespearean plays, leavened by an occasional thriller. Support for his company was universal, not only for the plays he presented but also for McMaster himself, an actor of commanding presence. 'Star quality', it is called. Few actors have it. Anew McMaster was one.

There was something cavalier about his acting, a delight in

performance for its own sake. His style was broad, a style now outdated by the camera and the microphone. An acting technique, like fashion, has its season and soon it is last year's garment. The style of Garrick or Irving, great actors of the past, if offered today would be laughed off the stage. But style is only style. New technology brings change, proper acoustics shrink declamation to intimacy, the camera creates new rules. Were he in his prime today, McMaster would as comfortably command his audience in the contemporary style as he did when I first saw him act seventy years ago. His forte was Shakespeare; *Hamlet, The Merchant of Venice* and *Macbeth* the most popular of the plays. Some marvel that Shakespeare drew audiences in small towns. Why not? Shakespearean plays are as action-packed as a late-night thriller, and Mac was a star with a star's box-office appeal.

The school's matinee, always of a play on the Leaving Certificate course, was a feature of the week. Christian Brothers boys and convent seniors separated by wary teachers. Chatter and din, paper aeroplanes flying, whistles at an attractive actress. The words of the big soliloquies, memorised by rote for the exam, chanted with the actor delivering them. If he dared to pause, he was beaten to the next line by a hundred prompts.

Nowadays Shakespeare is regularly played in modern costume to emphasise present-day relevance. Not everyone agrees, forgetting that in Shakespeare's own day his plays were performed in the costume of the time. There was a limit, of course. When it was suggested to the great David Garrick that he perform *Macbeth* in a kilt, 'And have my audience laugh at me?' was his horrified reply.

Mac was not above throwing in a thriller to make the turnstiles click. High art, low art or no art at all, the theatre is a place of entertainment, be it a nail-swallower in the town square or high opera in

Covent Garden at a cost beyond the common man's purse. The public demands entertainment, and unsubsidised theatre must provide it or succumb.

A lasting memory of Mac is not from the theatre but of seeing him on the beach after a swim, near his home in Sandymount. I had gone there to borrow spot lamps, and no one was more generous than Mac when it came to offering a helping hand to small companies. He was absent when I arrived, and I was chatting to his wife, Marjorie, when I saw him running near the tide line. The glowing Adonis of his youth had not yet faded. He was so full of energy, so seemingly untouched by the years, that it was difficult to believe that he was nearing sixty.

Because of his wayward concentration, legends gathered around Mac like moths around a flame: how he was still in full view when he pulled up his period gown and yanked up his trousers, how he lost his lines in *Hamlet* and picked up from *Lear*, how he played Long John Silver in the National Boxing Stadium with a stuffed parrot stitched to his shoulder (I was there), a crutch, and *two* legs, the supposedly lost one encased in black. A typical story recounted that when he was being driven by car from *The Pageant of Saint Patrick* on the hill of Slane, still dressed in mitre and full canonicals, he blessed the applauding throng with all the solemnity of His Holiness from the balcony of Saint Peter's.

The bitter winter of 1947 was long remembered by those who experienced it. Dublin was snowbound for over two months. Cars were abandoned in the street and my fellow lodgers in the Kilronan Hotel in Adelaide Road clubbed together to buy newspapers to encourage the watery slack that passed muster for firing. At the time Mac was running seasons simultaneously in the Gaiety and the Gate. 'I had always dreamed of running the two theatres simultaneously,' he declared wryly when he literally paid the price of extreme weather, with audiences of twenty in the Gaiety and fewer in the Gate. In the Gaiety he went in front of the curtain to gather in the front rows the thin scatter of hardy souls who had braved the weather 'so that both you and the actors will enjoy the show better.'

The play was *The Cardinal*, a piece Mac had played on and off for twenty years. It was a full-blooded melodrama, offering Mac a flowing costume and highly charged soliloquies. Early in the action a murder is committed and the culprit confesses to the Cardinal, knowing that under the seal of Confession the Cardinal is sworn to silence. Suspicion falls on the Cardinal's younger brother, played by myself, and thus the plot thickens. Patrick Magee, playing the Chief of Police, arrives to arrest me. Mac, at full throttle, clutches me to his bosom, declaring that right will prevail and soon I will be free.

During one performance, from the depths of Mac's enfolding embrace I heard him whisper something to Magee. Offstage I asked Magee what he had said and Magee beckoned me to follow him to the bar for a brandy and then back again to the side of the stage.

Mac was declaiming a long soliloquy, railing against the dilemma forced on him by the Seal of Confession. It was a major speech, offering him the opportunity to sweep hither and thither, swirling his scarlet cloak. The setting was a striking arrangement of drapes and pillars, the upstage pillar touching a masking wing. Before the speech ended Magee was in position behind the pillar. Catching his eye, Mac swept to it with a great cry, leaned against it, and, his face concealed by an arm on which rested his forehead, his free arm extended behind the pillar, his hand at the ready. Into it Magee popped the brandy, and with the smoothest of movements Mac raised it to his lips, swallowed it in one, returned the glass, uttered another cry, and was once more in full stride, his cloak swirling like the aurora borealis . 'He's not a drinker,' Magee made sure to explain. 'The brandy was just fuel to keep him going on a cold night.'

It would be easy to dwell on Mac's theatrical eccentricities and overlook the fact that he was a genuinely gifted actor. Magee spoke of him with the highest admiration, particularly of those nights when he was 'on form' and some shabby hall in the-back-of-God-speed was graced by a star actor playing at the top of his bent. Magee knew what he was talking about: in the years ahead he would move to London and work with the best in the West End.

In his early years Mac was a star in Stratford and London. Why he abandoned such a career for the small towns of Ireland is hard to fathom. Some would have it that scandal clouded his retreat from England, but that is always the way when invention is readier to hand than fact. Others had a simpler explanation- that he wished to run his own company and found touring in Ireland an outlet for his artistic ambitions. Which is true is now of no account. The small and large towns of Ireland were inestimably richer for Mac's personality and the wealth of drama he presented.

No doubt he hacked it too long on tour, allowing boredom and mechanical repetition to dull his sharp edge. But even at that, his talent and personality lifted him a good broad cut above his fellows. He commanded attention, brought colour to routine lives, made a generation pause at a shop window, as my father did, and feel a ripple of excitement that Mac was due to visit the local town. No actor commanded the touring stage as he did, none was better known throughout Ireland or so affectionately remembered by the generation he entertained.

Among the crumpled sheets of newspaper abandoned in the bottom of an old touring skip consigned to the rubbish dump, I found critiques of the performance of *The Playboy* in Derry, sometime in the forties. The *Derry Standard* took the view that, 'Making full allowance for the almost abnormal way of life in some of these isolated self-contained communities in the west of Eire, it would be difficult to accept the behaviour of the characters as being typical of life anywhere in Eire. Having seen the play the Londonderry audience who did not relish it can understand the feelings of resentment it created in Dublin when first presented there. But to Ulster folk who know the sympathy the "man on the run" gets in both countries the theme is scarcely credible . . . . The language which, because it introduces the Deity all too frequently, was somewhat shocking to the ears of the audience, and it is hoped that it is also an exaggeration of the everyday speech of Western Eire . . . . Everyone knows the weakness of the female sex for the young vagabond of attractive personality, but the hero worship of a murderer is too farfetched . . . .'

The *Derry Standard* invited (The Reverend?) Dr R. E. G. Armattoe, 'who has visited most parts of Ulster and Eire and knows these countries very well', to give his opinion of the play, which was that 'Mr Synge in his title is not correct in my view. It should have been 'Playboy of Western Ireland.' It is true that women sympathise with criminals and failures and weaklings, but has Mr Synge not overdrawn this quality in women in this play? . . . . There is neither message nor moral purpose in the play, although it makes the point that Irish people theoretically condone crimes, but when brought face to face with them they recoil in horror from them. Types like Christopher Mahon will always appeal to women all over the world because they bring romance and unreality into the harshness of their lives . . . . The play should not have introduced the Deity and the names of the saints so many times. He had not found this true to life in his experiences in Eire, and he thought it tended to lower the dignity and respect people had for religious things.' One wonders which part of Eire he had visited.

Thus the reaction of Derry – or ought I say Londonderry? – in the late forties. How fundamentally different, one wonders, was it from the reaction of Dublin when the play was first produced in the Abbey? One notes the use of 'countries' to distinguish between north and south. If we southerners did not quite think of Northern Ireland as a different country, the Border was an Iron Curtain, the separation of the nation deep and apparently permanent. Once also notes that, in the opinion of the Derry reviewer, no doubt a man, that only women, the weak creatures, had sympathy for the vagabond, or could be seduced by his charms.

We from the South smiled when we read these notices. We understood the play. We were a liberal people. Ulster, Protestant Ulster at least, was a dour and prejudiced place. Not that we approved of tinkers, blacks, homosexuals, multi-married film stars, divorce, abortion, atheists and agnostics (whatever the difference), Pearse or Collins (depending on one's political affiliation), the Labour Party, Russia, the affectations of Rathgar or the common accents of the inner city, to mention but a few. We were a stable society, we supported the Catholic Church, we stayed married. At a later date when Hugh Leonard's *The Passion of Peter Ginty* took to the stage, we were amused, but we did not take too seriously Peter's cry that 'We're all right the way we are.' Little did we suspect the shake-up that lay ahead when radio became the talking shop of the nation and *The Late Late* filled our screens. Who then could foresee that Carnaby Street would shock parents with the flash of their daughters' legs and the thunder of *Top of the Pops* would drown out the family Rosary.

No reservations were in evidence when we played *The Playboy* in Pomeroy, a small town in Tyrone. When the fight broke out between Christy and his father, the audience cheered, and when Old Mahon reappeared after his second killing, the roof nearly came off. And so it was across the province: audience response telling as much about social and religious attitudes as the morning newspaper that drops through a Belfast letterbox.

From the Derry notices I am reminded that I was then John Cassin. I rejected the name Barry, thinking it in some way effeminate, and went, with the flourish of a first-year university student, through a phrase of reverting to my full name, John Finbar Cassin. This did not last long. Using a triple name was not yet in vogue. Married women were content to be Mrs Whatever, and a man with three names, or a double-barrelled surname, was dismissed as a pretentious snob.

I was on a tour of Northern Ireland at the time under the auspices of CEMA. The company was under the direction of Louis D'Alton, a popular Abbey playwright and a prominent figure in the Irish theatre of the forties and fifties. Among his successful plays were *The Man in the Cloak*, *This Other Eden*, *Lovers' Meeting* and *The Money Doesn't Matter*. For a time he directed in the Abbey and his touring company was permanently on the road. His marriage to Annie had broken up when I joined the company. His partner was Eithne Mulhall, vivacious, glamorous, half his age. They were ever hand-in-hand.

Three plays were toured, *Shadow and Substance* by Paul Vincent Carroll, *The Playboy*, and an unpretentious light comedy, *Mr Pim*

Passes By by A. A. Milne, dismissed by Louis as 'Mr Pimp Asses By'. Louis appeared only in *Shadow and Substance*, playing the aloof Canon Skerritt, who is humbled by the simple faith of his serving maid, Brigid. Phyllis Ryan, who created the part in the Abbey, played Brigid. The role demands simplicity and a burning faith. No actress I have seen in the intervening years has matched the lambent conviction of Phyllis. It was the first time we met and our friendship would last a lifetime, including more than twenty years of continuous work as a director for her company, Gemini Productions.

Phyllis played Pegeen in *The Playboy*, and I played opposite her as Christy. Louis solved the problem of my height, six feet three, by changing the line describing Christy as 'a small low fellow' to 'a long, skinny fellow'. Not even Synge is sacred when needs must. And so, because of the limitations of the company manpower, it was my good fortune to play one of the most exciting roles in Irish drama. Come to think of it, I did a reading of the part before being engaged for the tour, so I must have had something going for me.

Illsley/McCabe engaged me for a season of plays in Cork. Joining the company for two of the plays was Esme Biddle, once a leading lady in Stratford but no longer appearing on the Dublin stage or touring with McMaster. My earliest memory of her was when she played Portia to Mac's Shylock in a school's matinee of *The Merchant of Venice* in Monaghan. She was tall. She moved with grace. Her voice was melodious.

We met when Frank O'Donovan, a leading comedian of the time, subsidised a tour which featured his daughter, Derry. When we were introduced, Esme beamed. 'A leading lady,' she declared, 'must have someone taller than herself to play opposite.' The tour was brief. Halfway through the second week, Frank was at the back of the hall with Ian Priestley-Mitchel, Esme's partner. 'Doesn't the set look beautiful?' Ian said. 'There are ten people out front,' Frank snapped. We closed on Saturday.

I next met Esme when Ian was directing an amateur production of *The Ghost Train* for a Sunday night in the Gaiety. I was summoned to his and Esme's flat in Mountjoy Square to discuss a backstage job. Esme served tea and cake with all the elegance of m'Lady in a West End success. Her chat was of Ivor, dear Ivor, and of Noël – Novello and Coward – meteors in the starry firmament of the West End. It was easy to believe that in sunnier days, when she played Shakespeare in Stratford, she had touched the ambit of the great ones. Her laugh was nervous, her smile uncertain, and it was all too easy to sympathise with her failed hopes and dreams, to believe that, had things been different, her stage might have been the West End, not the small towns of Ireland and the anonymity of Mountjoy Square.

Heads shook when the word went out that she had been engaged for the Cork season. Surely Stanley and Leo knew her reputation? Why had they taken such a chance? But in rehearsal it was easy to see why they had cast her as Mrs Smith in the thriller *Suspect*. She had presence. She dominated.

The plot revolved around the mystery of whether or not Mrs Smith was a notorious, unproven, axe-murderess of a previous generation – Lizzie Borden leaped to mind – but by the end of Act Three all fears had been allayed. Family and friends departed, and Mrs Smith was alone. Then the final twist. In a swirling fog she appeared outside the French window, seized an axe and, as the curtain fell, crashed it time after time into a tree trunk. Esme got excellent notices and it seemed that the gamble had paid off.

A new play opened on the second Monday, and all went well until the middle of the week. I was stage manager and it was my job to check that the cast were in place half an hour before the show, by knocking on dressing room doors and awaiting a reply. On the Wednesday or Thursday I did the usual round, calling, 'Half-an-hour, please,' and as usual, Esme replied with, 'Thank you, darling,' or something like that. Theatricality was her style.

Before 'Stand by' and 'Curtain up,' the traditional calls to commence a performance, I had not seen Esme, but there was nothing unusual in that: actors usually remain in their dressing rooms until the Inter-Com – in those days the call-boy's knock and 'Stand by please' – warns them that their entrance is approaching. From the stage management corner I could see the open door on the other side of the stage through which Esme would enter. She was in position as usual, and I suspected nothing until she came onstage. Her walk was unsteady, her first line slurred.

Stanley reacted immediately. He took Esme by the arm, guided her to the sofa, and seated her. The act struggled on, no one sure if Esme would take her cues or sit looking vacantly out front. Then came the moment when she must slap Stanley's face. With an effort she lurched to her feet and tried to focus. Desperately, Stanley shoved his face forward. She swung wildly, lost her balance and fell backwards, mercifully into the sofa behind her.

The interval was an agony of coffee and vomiting, the remainder of the performance an attempt to cover-up.

My dressing room was beside Esme's. When the final curtain fell, Stanley and Leo knocked on her door. She was reminded of promises made, of a contract broken. She was told that she had been offered a chance to redeem her reputation, and that never again would any management employ her. When Stanley and Leo left her dressing room, I could hear her piteous sobbing.

I should have gone to her to offer comfort – I know that now; it has troubled me ever since – but it was more than sixty-five years ago and I was callow and unsure. When she left the theatre I followed at a distance. Twice crossing St Patrick's Bridge, she clutched the parapet. She blundered up the steep hill to her digs off MacCurtain Street, her long black overcoat swinging, her hands outstretched against the wall to protect her from falling. The next morning she would waken to inconsolable humiliation.

At the end of the week she was gone and I would never see her again. Talent destroyed. A life destroyed.

I met Nora Lever in 1946 when we played in *The First Gentleman*, staged by Nigel Fitzgerald in the Cork Opera House. During the run we got talking, and decided to set up a company of our own. We had no money but, once on the road, we were confident that box office returns would see us through. So it was gather a company, rehearse, have a look at a map, pick an opening date, load the lorry and off we go.

First stop was Rathangan, County Kildare. Digs were difficult to find. The last company in town closed after a couple of nights, and did a midnight flit leaving landladies unpaid and borrowed furniture unreturned. Even a promise of money in advance cut no ice. Once bitten by the strolling players, the town was twice shy.

Beside the hall trickled a muddy stream cluttered with broken bedsteads and rusted bicycle wheels. I lobbed a stone into it. Ooze and slime and a nasty smell were the result. The omens were not propitious.

On opening night I waited at the hall entrance for the throngs to gather. From our record player blasted out the liveliest music we could muster from our collection of seventy-eights, jigs and reels and popular tunes to catch the ear of the town and encourage in an audience. Loudest of all rattled out a South American rhythm, 'The Green Cockatoo'. It rattled out in vain. Eight-fifteen came. Eight-twenty, eight-thirty, and the hall still empty. Don't worry, I told myself, in country places eight-thirty means nine, even nine-fifteen. For the third time 'The Green Cockatoo' rattled over the muddy stream, but by nine-thirty there was not a soul in sight. At ten I locked-up and the company straggled home, those who by cajoling, entreaty, money in the hand or weeping, had managed to negotiate a resting place. Two of the actors and myself were not so lucky; we must sleep in the hall.

It was a fitful night, wrapped in the front curtains to keep warm, the paddlings of the muddy stream slopping at the gable. Next morning, out of the goodness of his heart, the caretaker provided a pot of tea and slices of bread and butter. From somewhere a bag of tomatoes appeared, and we sat around a wickerwork basket, on it three mugs from props, a teapot, the bread and the tomatoes. Far off a rooster signalled that rural Ireland was rousing itself to another day.

Across our makeshift table my fellow actors faced each other in stony silence. One drew a tomato from the bag, glared at it, then viciously dug his teeth in it. The tomato exploded, cascading a stream of juice and pips across the table into the face of his companion. Speechless, the victim stared at the bag of tomatoes as if they, like the world itself, had turned against him. Slowly he left his chair and went outside. I waited for something to happen. I did not have to wait long. A bellow rent the air, loud enough to silence the distant rooster.

Later in day the local bellman was paid ten bob to cry our wares around the town. From street corners he croaked, 'In the Town Hall tonight, *Jane Eerie*. Half-eight sharp.'

At half-eight 'The Green Cockatoo' echoed once again from an empty hall. Around nine, a dozen or so arrived. When the curtain came down, only a handful remained.

Before leaving town I wired home. The details of that telegram need not be disclosed; suffice to say that it was in the mode of the apocryphal communication from an actor son to his doting parent, 'Another success, dear Mother. Please send a pound.' That humiliation suffered, I hired a lorry and we went our way.

We soldiered on. Business picked up. Our goal was Bangor, County Down, for a summer season. I had played there with Equity Productions, and when that company was disbanded Nora and I applied for the engagement. We would perform for two months, two plays a week – Monday to Wednesday/ Thursday to Saturday. No repeats, no Sunday performance. In Northern Ireland the Lord's Day was a time for church-going, not frivolity.

A summer season is relentless rehearsal, scripts ever in hand, lines, lines, lines. We set out on tour with seven plays, and rehearsed new ones on the road. When we reached Bangor we had built up a rep that would last for six or seven weeks, but inevitably we caught up on ourselves, and for the last couple of weeks we were memorising a new script every couple of days, what is known in the business as 'a line bash' – acting by numbers, no artistic reward and exhaustion thrown in.

From a blur of performances – comedy, tragedy, melodrama – I recall *Peg O' My Heart* – it never failed – *Jane Eyre*, adapted by Nora from an adaptation by someone else, thrillers numerous, *Hobson's*

Choice, a worthwhile comedy, and *Night Must Fall*, Emlyn Williams's masterly psychological thriller. *East Lynne* was resuscitated, and Maria Marten again fell victim to the designing William Corder. Wally Macken's *Mungo's Mansion* got an airing and caused protests because the word 'bloody' was used a number of times, something to think about when hardly a play reaches the stage nowadays without its leavening of 'fuck's. Radio and television substitute with the ridiculous 'bleep'; literature, film and stage take it in their stride. How, one wonders, is an author to portray certain levels of contemporary conversation without scattering the word around like snuff at a wake?

Actors prove time after time how rapidly they can work in an emergency, reminding me of those last couple of weeks in Bangor when it was death or glory on the barricades. But never again, Nora and I decided after a couple of Bangor seasons. Never again. We sought a base in Dublin, scoured the city and settled on the basement of 37 Lower Baggot Street, hence the name 37 Theatre Club. The stage measured twelve feet by eight. The auditorium consisted of four tiered rows of wooden benches. A full house was forty dedicated souls, in consideration of whose comfort we introduced cushions. They were homemade, inspiring the theatre critic Gabriel Fallon to remark that 'they were stuffed with nails and iron filings'.

Entry to 37 was down outside wooden stairs that showed their cracks when dry, and were like an ice rink in the rain. The box office was a hen-coop porch, where money was taken and a book signed to prove that 37 was a private club, not a place of public performance. Our adviser was none other than Cearbhall Ó Dálaigh, a regular patron, and future Attorney General, later to be President. Not that the powers that be gave us any trouble. Small transgressions were not worthy of the full majesty of the law. A different fate awaited 37.

At this time there were iron rules about not 'spoiling the illusion'. A curtain up before the show, or during an interval, would have been unthinkable, so in 37, despite the limitations of space, we erected front curtains and used realistic settings. Less than two feet separated the actors from the front row, and it was common for audience feet to be parked on the stage, a hazard for any actor unaccustomed to close-range work. One took a dive over high heels into the arms of an astonished lady. He probably planned it; he was that sort of chap.

Nora and I were not consciously avant garde. Our aim was to stage what we considered worthwhile plays not seen in the commercial theatres. I remember *Leonarda* by Bjørnstjerne Bjørnson, *The Rainmaker* by N. Richard Nash, *A Man with a Load of Mischief* by Clemence Dane, and *Love on the Dole* by Walter Greenwood and Ronald Gow, a play that dealt with trapped lives in industrial England. A number of interesting one-acts included *Portrait of a Madonna* by Tennessee Williams, in which Nora gave a performance of poignant sensitivity. Found on a library shelf was the touching *One Day More* by Joseph Conrad, and, to lighten an evening of one-acts, we included short pieces by Noël Coward.

We were fortunate in our set designers. With meticulous realism, Anne Yeats painted, one over the other, four layers of peeling wallpaper for *Portrait of a Madonna*. The result was remarkably atmospheric, even if we fretted offstage waiting for her to finish so that we might rehearse.

Our most imaginative designer was Tomás Mac Anna, bustling in with paints and brushes, his assistant Paddy Mooney at his side. I am astounded to remember that tiny 37 had his services for the princely sum of £1 a week for the run of the show. Such was his generosity, such was his enthusiasm. Tomás was a man to meet when the heart was troubled. If anyone could raise it, he could. Even allowing that the stage was small, the speed with which Tomás and Paddy worked was astonishing. Sometimes they were in and out in less than an hour, the flats transformed, nothing skimped, nothing slapdash. The sets painted by Tomás contributed greatly to the artistic success of 37.

Ruth Durley was one of our regular players. Only when she painted a dramatic series of black and white cloths for Elmer Rice's *The Adding Machine* did we learn that she was also a designer of talent.

The central figure in *The Adding Machine* is Mr Zero, an adding machine operator and hapless victim of technology. Frank Purcell, an actor who in other times might have been a full-time professional, played an impressive Zero, with Ruth Durley as his nagging wife. Jack Aronson, destined to have a big success in America with his one-man show on Dylan Thomas, played Shrdlu, and I learn from an old programme that Anna Manahan was 'A Head', whatever that was. I played Zero's sardonic, next-life guard, promising that forever he would operate 'a hyper-super adding machine with the great toe of his right foot.'

The play, written in the twenties, had been outstripped by Chaplin's *Modern Times*, but its study of man enslaved by the machine made it a worthwhile revival. The party scene is a chant of racial prejudice from a chorus of think-alike clones: Mr and Mrs Zero, Mr and Mrs One, Mr and Mrs Two, etc. 'Damn Niggers, damn Sheenies, damn Catholics,' and so on, is their chant. At rehearsal I noticed that one of the cast, while enthusiastic about the rest of the chorus, kept his mouth shut when he reached 'Damn Catholics'. I asked him why. He was a Catholic, he explained, and therefore could not say 'Damn Catholics'. I pointed out that he seemed happy enough to damn every other creed, to which he replied that damning

Catholics was different. I let it go. I knew a brick wall when I saw one, especially when it had broken glass on top.

Nora and I would have wished it otherwise, but casting only professional actors at professional rates was not possible in our tiny theatre. But no professional, if he or she was available, ever refused to play for the bus fare we offered. Anna Manahan was one of our regulars. Norman Rodway joined us when a friend spotted him in an amateur production and sent him along for an audition, and David Kelly had yet to make a run for the professional theatre when he first appeared in 37. The list is long: Pauline Delany, Martin Dempsey, Patrick Bedford, Helen Robinson, Dermot Kelly, and, not allowing the rickety stairs to deter them, senior players like Paul Farrell and Ann Penhallow. That these players were willing to appear in 37 I take as a compliment to the genuineness of our endeavour, and the serious attention we attracted from the critics.

Under stage management was the name of a jolly young woman named Margaretta D'Arcy, who would marry John Arden and storm the world with strident socialism, and on a number of cast lists figured John Jordan, academic and writer. Dropping in to chat was a young Edna O'Brien, as yet to flutter the dovecot of Irish respectability with *The Country Girls* and *Girls in Their Married Bliss*, and heckling with the best of them in a noisy crowd, when we played *Love on the Dole*, was Jack Keyes Byrne, who would emerge as the international playwright Hugh Leonard.

Retrospection casts a romantic glow over grinding work. Putting a play onstage in 37 was more than acting or directing; it was building and erecting sets, it was adapting biscuit tins into makeshift spot lamps, it was homemade costumes. Shoestring enthusiasm would have waned had we not won serious attention from the press, and developed the confidence to book regular seasons in the Gate. The company also appeared in the Olympia and the Gaiety. In the latter we presented *The Innocents*, a stage version of Henry James's *The Turn of the Screw*, a performance notable for the playing of the children, Flora and Miles, by Elizabeth Robbins and John Keogh, who would later hit the headlines as one of the musical group The Green Beats.

So many plays did 37 perform that dates and venues merge. Theatre is a transient art. When the curtain descends on the last night, no monument of brass remains, but it is gratifying when someone recalls a performance from the past, that all has not been in vain. I received a letter from a gentleman saying that from forty years of theatre-going he would not forget *The Adding Machine* or *Under Milk Wood*. One cannot hope for more.

The move to 37's second home was unplanned. Word came backstage after a performance that a gentleman out front claimed he had a suitable premises available in O'Connell Street. It sounded too good to be true. O'Connell Street. City centre. But it was true enough. Harry Dillon, a jeweller, had made the offer. His premises were three doors from O'Connell Bridge. Over his shop was a vacant mezzanine floor. One look and we made up our minds.

A builder was contacted, a stage erected and the auditorium raked to hold around two hundred. We dress rehearsed in a blizzard of sawdust and a barrage of last minute hammering. I did not know until next day, when I sat on the back of a seat and the whole row teetered, that our distinguished first-night audience of city fathers, politicians and ambassadors had unwittingly risked life and limb in rows of seats held upright by no more than a couple of ground screws.

My father, John Cassin, in his First World War uniform. He served in France from 1914 to 1918.

With my parents, John and Lilian, and a friend at the bridge at Killaloe, 1930

Beside my father's bicycle on the bridge at Killaloe, 1930

University student, Cork 1943

Barry and Nancy, Wedding Day,
16 May 1961

Patrick Galvin (right) discusses his play
And Him Stretched with Barry Cassin
and Leila Doolan

Barry in George Bernard
Shaw's *Arms and the Man*
with Lister Skelton and
Denis Brennan, 1944

Arms and the Man with
Daphne Carroll, 1944

Anna Manahan in full flight

Barry while artistic director for
the Irish Theatre Company

Maurice Meldon,
author of *Aisling*

Barry as John Proctor and Ronnie
Masterson as Elizabeth Proctor in the first
Irish production of Arthur Miller's *The Crucible*

Marie Kean as Maggie
and Liz Davis as Katie in
the first production of
John B. Keane's
Big Maggie, 1969

Ray McAnally and Barry in dress
rehearsals for the first production
of *The Field* in 1965. This production was also directed by Barry.

A break in dress rehearsals
for *The Field*

Ray McAnally as Bull McCabe
in the first performance of
The Field

Ray McAnally

Phyllis Ryan

As Colonel Pickering in George Bernard Shaw's *Pygmalion* at
the Lyric Theatre, Belfast, 1996

We opened with a double bill, *Doña Clarines* by the Quintero brothers and Synge's *The Tinker's Wedding*. I would learn that this was the first production in Dublin of *The Tinker's Wedding*, which, if correct, astonished me. Was it because the tinkers bundled a priest into a sack that the play was refused a Dublin stage? Was there a fear that it would be greeted by clerical disapproval and the outrage of right-thinking people which had greeted *The Playboy* and, many years later, O'Casey's *The Bishop's Bonfire* and *The Ginger Man* by J. P. Donleavy? This was a time when Ireland did moral outrage. And did it big. An extreme of prudishness was reached at the Father Mathew Hall when an amateur group presented *Juno and the Paycock*, with Mary suffering from consumption, rather than having a baby, and it was more than urban myth that amateur actresses refused the part of Mary through fear of what local gossip might imply.

In O'Connell Street we were in continuous production, and could pay small – very small – professional fees. To do so, we had to keep an eye on the box office. We alternated the light with the serious; *The Mollusc* with the bitter anti-war play *The Man Outside*, Jean Cocteau's *The Eagle Has Two Heads* with Sacha Guitry's *Don't Listen, Ladies*, Coward's *Blithe Spirit* with *Iníon Rí Dhún Sobhairce* by Séamus Ó Néill. We had not planned to present a play in Irish, but through the good offices of Tomás Mac Anna we received a grant from the Abbey that made the production possible.

The Man Outside by Wolfgang Borchert came early in 1953, a first production of the play in Ireland. With Norman Rodway as my alter ego, I played Beckman, the disillusioned soldier returned from the war to a shattered Germany. That December the *Evening Herald* critic, John Finnegan, requested a photograph, and it had all the keen pleasure of the unexpected when I was given honourable mention as

Best Actor in his annual review of the theatrical year.

Our most important production in O'Connell Street was *Aisling* by Maurice Meldon. It satirised romantic Ireland dead and gone but still revered by politicians, clergy and diverse patriots determined to wrap the nation in the patriotic green, white and yellow of compulsory Irish. By their reckoning, Cathleen ni Houlihan simpered modestly across the half-door, *céilidh*-danced, and cycled home with the messages, casting an eye neither right nor left at the lusty lads who wolf-whistled at the crossroads. She may even have considered entering a convent. Maurice Meldon's Cathleen was a far different maiden. She moved through the play under various guises; was Gráinne and Maeve by turn, was rescued in 1916, and, in the play's final irony, auctioned off in the present day – the present day, of course, being the 1950s when the play was first staged. On her wanderings she encountered the poet Padraigeen Mullarkey, so obviously a caricature of Patrick Kavanagh – although Maurice would never admit it – that I played him in tweeds and used an exaggerated rural accent. Kavanagh arrived to see the play, but apart from smoking throughout (against the rules, but who dare challenge him?) and muttering loudly now and then, took no further action in the proceedings.

After one performance Padraic Colum hung on for a chat. He was impressed by the play and wished to meet the author, but, typically, Maurice had slipped away and was nowhere to be found. He was a retiring man, never one to dominate the conversation, but his reclusiveness concealed a keen observation and wry humour. In *Aisling* he acted under the pseudonym of Art O'Phelan, but, far from interfering in the production, he had to be forced into an answer when a question arose about the text. It was as if, having written the play, he had withdrawn from it. His reserve in company was neither uncivil nor a retreat, it was his watchtower from which to observe and take note. His death, aged only thirty-two, his talent only coming to flower, was the tragic result of a fall from his bicycle on his way home from work. One can only speculate about the direction his writing would have taken had he lived, but *Aisling* remains to remind us of a unique talent silenced too soon.

A year after opening in O'Connell Street, our Christmas offering, an Aldwych farce, was still running when the Dublin Corporation fire chief paid us a visit. He pointed out that there was only one exit from the premises, a door at the back of the auditorium opening onto narrow steps leading down to O'Connell Street. The stage and the raked auditorium were built of wood, the scenery was of wood and canvas. Lighting was primitive. Leads hung everywhere. Nothing was fireproofed. We protested that we were sensible people, that the oil stoves we used to heat the auditorium were turned off when the audience arrived, and that there was a no smoking rule. We did not inform the fire chief that the box on which he was sitting had been hastily upturned to conceal a can of paraffin when we were warned of his approach. We had deceived ourselves that, by operating as a club, we were immune from the attentions of the fire authorities. It is also true that at the time many public places – theatres, hotels, pubs, dance halls, which by modern standards would be deemed fire risks – operated without hindrance. They, at least, had a number of exits, we had but one. Moreover, 37 was no longer an obscure studio holding an audience of forty; it was a city centre theatre capable of seating two hundred, and the authorities dared not turn a blind eye. Within a few weeks we were ordered to close.

Packing up in O'Connell Street, I was resentful. I did not accept that the theatre was a major fire risk. It was not until the Stardust tragedy in 1981, when forty-eight young people died in a ballroom fire, that I asked myself how I would have felt had a fire broken out in 37, trapping audience and actors. Stardust starkly awakened the public and the authorities to the dangers of fire. The memory haunts the nation still.

The closing of O'Connell Street could have been the end of 37, but we struggled on. We scanned the To Let columns of the newspapers. We advertised under Wanted. We tramped the city to view basements, lofts, abandoned warehouses and bicycle sheds. Some were too big, others too small, some too remote, some beyond repair. Just when hope was fading, a phone call invited us to view a basement that might suit. The address was 36 Lower Baggot Street, next door to our first home. We had come full circle. We were back to the grind, but a base was ours and we were doing our independent thing. With an effort of memory I recall *The Dark at the Top of the Stairs* by William Inge and *The Rainmaker*, but the jewel in our crown was that 37 was the first company to present Arthur Miller's *The Crucible* in Dublin.

How it came about has always puzzled me. Allowing that in the fifties the Abbey rarely looked beyond its national boundaries, and that Longford Productions concentrated on the classics, I would have expected Illsley/McCabe or, more likely, Edwards/Mac Liammóir, who had staged *Death of a Salesman*, to be interested in *The Crucible*. Neither was. It could be that they did not see the play as good box office. If so, they had a point, for in spite of good notices when we staged it, especially for Ronnie Masterson as Elizabeth, the house was not full in tiny 37 or in the Olympia when we transferred at the invitation of Stanley Illsley.

That Miller was attacking Senator McCarthy and his anti-

Communist witch hunt seemed to pass unnoticed. McCarthyism was an American phenomenon far from our shores, and few seemed to connect Miller's Salem with McCarthy's crusade. In truth, in those fervidly anti-Communist times more than a few would have supported McCarthy when he named Hollywood writers and film stars as Communist sympathisers. Were not writers always suspect? Did we not ban some of our own? The lives of film stars were blatantly immoral, so who was surprised that they were also Red?

A generation on, with astonishing rapidity, through the power of radio and television, the dead grip of censorship was loosened, the old self-satisfied provincialism that had bounded Ireland with its holier-than-thou certainties was challenged, and the stifling dominance of the Catholic Church was side-lined. An economic boom would push the borders farther back, and with money to jingle in purse or pocket a young generation saw little reason to touch the forelock or bow the knee. McCarthy was consigned to history, and *The Crucible* was received with enthusiasm when, in the one year, it was staged by the Abbey, Red Kettle of Waterford and the Lyric, Belfast.

On a visit to America I visited Salem, and the house of one of the judges who had presided at the trials. It bore no scars to mark it as a place of evil. It was an ordinary house where ordinary people lived. So too were the streets, preserved as they were in 1692, no gaudy signs, no witch hats for the kids, just quiet streets where God-fearing citizens walked. On those streets the import of the play was even more forceful than in the theatre. A question came to mind that troubled me: had I been a citizen of Salem in those days of zealotry and trepidation, would I have supported the liberal Proctor or been swept along on the tide of the hanging Danforth? Hindsight makes the answer obvious, but at the time . . . ?

The 37 Theatre Club operated from 36 Lower Baggot Street for a year before the building was sold to a business and we were ordered to leave. On the advice of Charlie Starkie, solicitor and friend, we refused to shift. Nothing happened immediately and we were rehearsing *The Return* by Bridget Boland, with Ronnie Masterson in the lead, when Nora went early one morning to the theatre. Immediately she rang in distress to say the place had been taken apart. And so it had. Seating had been unscrewed, the raked floor and stage dismantled. No damage had been done to effects or properties. We had received an unorthodox notice to quit. On Charlie's advice we held on. The tabloid press cottoned on to us. *Penniless Artists Resist Big Business*, or some such sob-stuff, made a good headline. The premises were locked by the new owners and on Charlie's instructions a photographer was summoned to click his camera when I climbed over the railings to break into what we claimed was our premises. 'For publicity,' Charlie said. 'We need sympathy on our side when it comes to a court case.'

When I entered and looked around, I was shocked. Not so much that the place had been dismantled, but that the knife of eviction had slid fatally in. Our base was gone. It was a sort of death.

Ernest Wood, renowned defender of the little man, was briefed by Charlie. He was an agreeable fellow, full of glee. He said his piece at the hearing while Nora and I sat in the solemn surroundings of the court, not centre-stage at our own case but bit players waiting in the wings. Without consultation we were told that a settlement had been agreed. For a few hundred quid, if I remember – we certainly didn't make our fortunes. That was that. Over and out. No cameras clicked when we were leaving court. We'd had our fifteen minutes of tabloid fame.

I had never thought of 37 as a highroad to international fame and for-tune. I had hoped to establish a company that would play in Dublin and on tour. That dream was now shattered. I was back in the pack, sunk without a trace. When Gerard Healy offered me a job as stage manager with a company that would play in London, I accepted. I had no wish to be a stage manager but I saw little chance of regular work with the established Dublin companies. The Edwards/Mac Liammóir company and Longford Productions were veritable closed shops, and acceptance into the Abbey company required fluency in Irish, which I had not. So it was goodbye Dublin. Goodbye Ireland. Hail emigra-tion to join the ambitious and the dispossessed who had gone before.

The company I joined was an offshoot of the Players' Theatre, which some years previously had a brief career commencing with *The Black Stranger* by Gerard Healy, commissioned for the Famine com-memoration of 1947. It ran in the Gate with Liam Redmond out-standing as the father, symbol of a stricken nation's endurance and tenacity. A season followed in the Olympia, with plays by Redmond and Seamus de Faoite, whose play touched on incest, a daring theme for the time. The season failed and no more was heard of a company that had promised much.

Some years later, Healy, Redmond and Helen O'Malley – founder members of the Players' Theatre – joined forces again to present O'Casey and Synge in the Lindsey Theatre, Notting Hill Gate. The season was a triumph for Redmond, his performances as Captain Boyle in *Juno and the Paycock*, Fluther in *The Plough and the Stars*, and Martin Doul in *The Well of the Saints* winning the highest praise from the London critics.

Throughout the season I was dissatisfied. Stage management was not acting, was not directing. When the season ended I hung on in Notting Hill Gate in the hope of finding work, until a shortage of money forced me to move to a flat near Latimer Road tube station. The address was Blechynden Street, a name as unenticing as the rooms I occupied on the top floor. On street level was a laundry where female Irish voices threatened violence if the missing bag-wash did not fucking turn up tomorrow, and male Irish voices disturbed the early-to-bed English with late-night chorusing of *I'll take you home again, Kathleen*. And kept me awake counting, for the hundredth time, the chimneypots outlined against an alien sky and listening to passing tube trains that led to nowhere I wanted to go.

I occupied two rooms, a bedroom on one side of the upstairs landing, a living room on the other. On the landing stood a gas stove and a pockmarked sink. Good enough for one who must live skinny and endure the cold deep into November when frost drove me to order coal, and count out a daily allowance lump by lump.

It was not that I did not look for work. I wrote to every possible source. I tramped agents' stairs, despising those who threw my photograph in a drawer without looking at it, sometimes without looking at me. Surprisingly, I was interviewed by one of the biggest agents in London. Had I known that he handled only film stars and featured players I would not have thought it worth my time to write, but he gave me half an hour, which was more than could be said for some of his lesser brethren – one of whom, a producer in the BBC, sat behind his desk fingering indifferently through my CV. Prominent was my photograph as Beckmann in *The Man Outside*, with John Finnegan's assessment in the *Evening Herald* that it was the best acting performance of the year. The gentleman looked it over. 'Of course,' he said, 'it might have been the only part you ever played well.' I was as yet too mannerly to answer him with a four-letter word.

Solitary days without work grind down the spirit. It was a relief to don my Sunday best – I had one decent suit – and walk in the West End, a keep-the-heart-up exercise when the alternative was to stare down from my top floor window at a featureless grey street, at head-scarves and curlers, at twists of cigarette smoke, at umbrellas and soaked gabardines hurrying to the tube, and at a grossly fat man who scowled from a window like a flatulent Buddha.

I was a poor grafter. I could have learned from Jack MacGowran, who said, 'Go back to Dublin? If I have to starve I'll buy drinks in the right bars for the right people until I'm established here.' Or from Patrick Magee when I bumped into him in Charing Cross Road, 'Go back to what? To touring with Mac?' Both stayed. Both conquered.

A friend who taught Irish dancing thought to cheer me up by inviting me to a concert in Kilburn. A tricolour was hung above the stage. The hall was filled with raucous young men and ruddy girls not yet made sallow by the city smog. Jigs and reels were danced by teams bestrewn with medals like competitors at the Father Mathew Feis. 'Amhrán na bhFiann' rounded off the evening.

I found it all *Mother Macree*, as kitsch as dancing at the crossroads for American tourists. What I failed to understand was that I was listening to a cry of loneliness from those who sought to bring their Ireland abroad with them. Solitary days on the top floor in Blechynden Street would soon teach me something of the anchorless loneliness of the emigrant, but, that evening, far from wishing to revel in nostalgia, I resisted, resolved that if I was forced to remain in London I would do all in my power to avoid becoming a ghetto person. I would not strive to be a Londoner but I would be prepared to meet the city halfway.

Blechynden Street taught me to sympathise with those who sank into frowsy squats and the destitution of cardboard city. I did not cry the Tory cry of 'Get on your bike', but I counted my lucky stars that no matter how broke I was, I could swallow my pride and write home for rescue. Nor was I one of those with dependants back home who relied on the weekly money order, in a time when the mail boat was a certain transport abroad for thousands in a country unable to support its population. A west of Ireland parish priest once showed me his parish book. In house after house were the names of ageing brothers and sisters. The young were gone, many uneducated, fit only for the pick and shovel of McAlpine's Fusiliers. At least my priest friend did not proclaim unctuously, as did others of his cloth, that 'the good Irish boys and girls will spread the Faith in heathen England.'

In London I appeared in a television ad for Hammerton's Stout, featuring the boxer Freddie Mills, who had considerable difficulty enunciating the slogan 'Have a Hammerton's for Zest', and was fun enough to laugh at himself. More seriously, I played in a couple of television plays and in a production of *Juno and the Paycock* in the Theatre Royal, Windsor. Barbara Mullen, who starred in the film *Man of Aran*, played Juno, but it is not her name that brings Windsor to mind. Also in the cast was Edward Mulhare, who last figured in this memoir declaiming Shakespeare to fellow lodgers at the dining table of a Dublin digs. Towards the end of the run he announced that when he finished in Windsor, he was due in Edinburgh, to take over in a play destined for the West End. Because of the short notice, he would be given two weeks to settle in before it was decided whether or not he would be retained for the London run.

I took his story with a grain of salt. Edward's tales of success just around the corner were too often followed by denunciation of a blundering agent who had made a mess of things. But this time, his story was no fantasy. He went to Scotland, succeeded in the part and was retained for the London run. And there was more. Much more. What followed was the fairy tale stuff that gives perpetual hope to the humblest walk-on. Edward's next stop was Broadway, to take over from Rex Harrison in *My Fair Lady*. Top of the bill, his name in lights, and, ahead, the television series *The Ghost and Mrs Muir*. Achieving stardom had taken Edward a little longer than the ten years he gave himself when declaiming Shakespeare to a flabbergasted dining table, but he'd made it, and none, I am sure, was less surprised than he was.

During my year in London, I picked up enough work to live, or at least exist. Very good, I was told, you're getting a foot in. I didn't want a foot in. I had learned to my surprise that Ireland was injected more deeply into my being than I would have suspected. Not with nationalism or republicanism but with the fields and country towns, the canals of Dublin and walking home in security when the hour was late, and, I admit, the confidence bred of being known in Dublin, while in London I was another faceless face in the faceless multitude of an indifferent city. For all the poverty of the time, Dublin in the fifties, self-satisfied, provincial and inflated with moral certitude, was a mollycoddling place where I could be comfortably hard-up among my friends.

A memory of my time in London was of attending a production of *Hedda Gabler* in Hammersmith. John Gielgud directed, Peggy Ashcroft played Hedda, and appearing as Judge Brack was Michael Mac Liammóir. At the time I was rehearsing in the Arts Theatre for a production of *Saint Joan*. During a break a young man approached me. He wanted to know all about this impressive Irish actor, Mac Liammóir, who was playing in Hammersmith. 'We must get him over to London,' the young man said. I told him how unlikely that was, surprising the young man that an actor of Mac Liammoir's talent would choose Dublin rather than London as his base. Dublin is Michael's home, I told him; he operates from there. The young man was disappointed. His name was Peter Hall.

Saint Joan, for which I was rehearsing, launched Siobhán McKenna into international stardom. The intensity of her emotion, the spirituality she brought to the part of Joan, and her Irish peasant quality took London by storm. Overnight she was a star, and it was no small thing to hear the nightly thunder of applause that greeted her curtain call.

Throughout her career I saw Siobhán play many parts. My memories of her are framed by the Saint Joan of her youth and her Old Woman in Tom Murphy's *Bailegangaire*, her last performance before her untimely death. Her Irishness is what I remember, an Irishness of my early years, of country places and country people, of my aunt's open hearth and farmhouse kitchen, of a marionette dancing to the lilting of a jolly woman in a Monaghan border village, and of the dazzling colours of a kingfisher flashing under a bridge. That Ireland stirred in me when I played the Executioner in *Saint Joan* and stood close to Siobhán in the trial scene. It sent me nightly to the tube accepting that I was as alien in this foreign land as those gathered for the Irish Night in Kilburn.

After a year I said goodbye without regret to Blechynden Street. And to my landlord. When he called for his rent, he wasted no time on chit-chat. It was knock, collect, sign the rent book and go. During our brief encounters I had learned, or guessed, something about him, and had a point to make. 'I hope you found me a good tenant.'

'No complaints.'

'I'm going back to Dublin on Monday.'

'Dublin?' He was suspicious.

'I'm Irish. You said I was a good tenant. I hope that in future you will think well of my fellow countrymen.'

'I won't. If I'd known you were Irish, I'd have told you to leave.'

At least the bastard was honest.

With relief I saw Dun Laoghaire appear over the horizon. Nora was waiting, and it seemed obvious that we would pick up the threads of 37.

Which we did, playing regularly in the Gate and the Olympia. Many of the performances have faded into the blurry mishmash of the past, but occasionally the Jack-in-the-Box of memory is sprung by a dog-eared programme or a chance remark. *A Moon for the Misbegotten* by Eugene O'Neill and *Under Milk Wood* by Dylan Thomas come to mind. In *A Moon for the Misbegotten* I played opposite Anna Manahan, and must record that during my many years in the theatre I met few so totally dedicated as Anna. Intensity invested every aspect of her days, and this intensity marked her, even when very young, as one who would reach the top of her profession. As I sat out front, when she played in Martin McDonagh's *The Beauty Queen of Leenane*, my mind went back to our fit-up days when Anna, in full flight, grabbed a flat for support and the canvas walls teetered. And to the occasion in a seance scene when the other three actors unkindly levitated the table with their knees, causing her to panic. But if I smile at these memories, I also recalled the invaluable contribution Anna made to 37 with a series of impressive performances, and to the countless roles she played with Phyllis Ryan's Gemini Productions.

Few shows leap to mind as readily as *Under Milk Wood*. It had not been performed in Dublin when Nora and I sought the rights in 1957. Dylan Thomas's agent, Margery Vosper, had never heard of us. Who were we? What was our average audience? In what theatre would we stage the production? Twice she would have ended the correspondence but we would not give up. Request followed plea, followed expostulation, until more than a year after our first enquiry she wrote, 'You seem so enthusiastic about *Under Milk Wood* that I will allow you to perform it.'

Originally written as 'A play for voices', *Milk Wood* was given a first reading in America by a group of actors, each of whom played a number of parts, with Thomas himself as the First Narrator. To bring the seaside town to life, for our performance in the Gate, we cast about thirty-five players (I tell no lie) – the core professional, the townspeople and children amateur.

There was rarely a rehearsal without one or two of the crowd missing. Amateurs are not professionals; the theatre is their hobby, not their way of life. That I understood, but I was still burning-enthusiast enough not to fathom how anyone would not think the world well lost for the sake of a show, and in the heat of production had to bite my tongue because it was badminton night, or mother's night at the pictures, or Sodality night in Saint Michael the Archangel's. Even at the dress rehearsal, one was missing. But on the first night all were present and correct, and for the run of the play, hail, rain, snow, film buff mother or the demands of sanctity, none missed a performance.

By the standards of the time the show was difficult. Nowadays the computer would render the technical demands rather easy, but in the fifties it was a nightmare to alternate twenty discs on a single turntable in the half-dark of a crowded prompt corner. So too with lighting. The Gate was then equipped with thirty or so dimmers spread along the wall at stage left. The operator could not see the stage and relied on hand signals from the stage manager to take his cues. When a cue was complicated, he used hands, slotted sticks devised to operate selected dimmers simultaneously, and even his feet. In extremes he was known to tie a string around a particular dimmer and pull it with his teeth. Such heroics performed by Arthur Jones and Eric Doyle have passed unnoticed in the annals of the theatre.

A feature of the show was the magnificent set designed by Tomás Mac Anna, a series of ramps sweeping from the town down to the shore where Nogood Boyo's boat was moored. From a chain of warm memories I see Anna Manahan's colourful Rosie Probert, Dermot Tuohy's Captain Cat, the benign Eli Jenkins of Robert Somerset, the Lily Smalls of Margaret O'Dalaigh, and, when Milk Wood day was drawing to a close, I hear the bawdy pub song 'Come and Sweep My Chimney'.

At the final curtain on the first night the company was given a standing ovation. Nowadays standing ovations are run-of-the-mill, but in the fifties a standing ovation was a rarity. When the audience rose to its feet at the final curtain, I could scarcely believe me eyes. But I could have walked on water.

I played the Narrator, and from the opening line was part of Llareggyb, so immersed that I was neither surprise nor alarmed on the night when, out of the corner of my eye, I saw Dylan Thomas sitting on the stage a short distance from me. I am not psychic. I do not hallucinate. But he was there.

Illusion is an aspect of reality, a double-image of consciousness. I was at once an actor onstage in live performance and simultaneously

in the company of a poet some years dead. I felt no distress, no eeri-
ness. Rather, I felt that his presence approved of the performance of
his play, and that was as rewarding as the excellent press notices for
the production.

For a couple of minutes I had no lines to speak. While I remained
silent, I knew that he would stay, but if I looked in his direction he
would be gone. And so it was, until my cue arrived and I must move
to where he sat. And when I did, he was gone. As I knew he would
be. I felt no sense of loss. I was elated that he had come to keep me
company for a little while.

Imagination, that's all it was, but, even still, at the mention of
Dylan Thomas's name I do not bring to mind his photograph or even
Under Milk Wood. I remember that once he sat with me on the stage
of the Gate, and that together we listened to his words. And that was
as good as if it really happened.

With Dave Atkins as Alfred Doolittle and
Niall Cusack as Professor Higgins in
Pygmalion - Lyric Theatre, Belfast, 1996

Working

Barry as ninety-nine-year-old Noel Sloan in *Lengthening Shadows* by Graham Reid. Lyric Theatre, Belfast, 1995

With Julia Deardon as Carol in *Lengthening Shadows* by Graham Reid

Nancy with daughter-in-law,
Mary, and grandson, Eoghan

At Salmon – country gentleman!

Nancy at home

Twelve Angry Men by Reginald Rose, Lane Productions. Back row from left: Pat Nolan, Michael Merrit , Sean Power, Terry Byrne (director). Second row from left: Pascal Scott, William Morgan Jr, Joe Hanley, Eamon Glancy, Paul Bennett, Tony Coleman, Peter Vollebregt. Third row from left: Patrick Joseph Byrnes, Hugh McCusker, Barry Cassin.

Barry as the Grey Man with Derbhle Crotty
as Cauth Carmody in *The Dandy Dolls* by
George Fitzmaurice. Peacock Theatre, 2004

Barry with his five children and their partners. Back row from left: Donagh, Jeanne,
James, Sinead, Tom, Mary and Philip. Front row: Anne, Barry, Lilian and Andrew.

John B. Keane outside his pub in Listowel

With Eugene McCabe, author of
Pull Down a Horseman

Barry and Seamus Heaney at the opening
night of Heaney's *The Burial at Thebes*,
Peacock Theatre, 2008

Kevin Flood, Barry and Tom Murphy at the opening night of
Seamus Heaney's *The Burial at Thebes*, Peacock Theatre, 2008

Barry with Neil Jordan during filming of
Byzantium, 2012

Barry and Saoirse Ronan during filming
of Neil Jordan's *Byzantium*, 2012

4

Let me recall the first time I saw *Waiting for Godot*, in 1955, in the Pike Theatre run by Alan Simpson and Carolyn Swift in Herbert Place, a short distance from 37. We met in the College Players' small theatre in Limerick, when I played there for a season managed by Ward Lloyd and Catherine Wainwright. Members of the company were Denis Brennan, in his early twenties and already a splendid character actor, and Daphne Carroll. Soon they would marry and, with their children, Stephen, Barbara, Catherine, Jane and Paul, become Ireland's first theatrical family. (I do not forget the Cusack sisters, but their work was mainly in England with nothing like the Brennans' influence on Irish theatre.)

During the season Cyril Cusack was invited to play in *Arms and the Man*. I had seen him act many times and marvelled at his naturalistic style, so underplayed that a couple of times in rehearsal I thought he had made a casual remark when he had actually spoken a line of script. I questioned him about the difference between playing on stage and acting for camera. His explanation was memorable, 'Onstage you act. Before a camera you think.'

Observing him during rehearsal I learned much about the subtleties of acting, as well as learning how to row when we found ourselves aboard a boat on the Shannon in the small hours. Where had the boat come from? How had we boarded it? How did we get away with it? Of such mysteries nothing remains but the memory of pulling along the broad majestic Shannon far from the world and its petty concerns. That is, if it ever really happened, for there were lost nights that season, when 'going home by rail' was a phrase learned in the high jocularity of pub talk, a euphemism for progress in the small hours by working hand after hand along the railings over the basements in O'Connell Street. By now it is all so distant that it might have happened to someone else. In a way it did, to a young man laughing all the way, fit for rehearsal next morning, boasting about how much he had consumed the previous night, one who found companionship only in fellow drinkers. In time he would be found out, but we will come to that.

Directing the season was Alan Simpson, assisted by his first wife Carolyn, who would be a lifelong friend until her death in 2003. She and Alan would convert a garage in Herbert Lane into a pocket theatre – wings, flies, lighting bar, everything – to form the Pike Theatre, and administer an exciting injection into theatrical Dublin. This they did most notably with the first Dublin production of *Waiting for Godot*, in 1955, and with a series of off-the-beaten-track plays, until the ludicrous rumpus surrounding *The Rose Tattoo*.

I have always regretted that I did not accept Alan's invitation to play in *Godot* when he offered me the part of Lucky. I had just landed a permanent job in the Radio Éireann Repertory Company, and permanent work after a flat-broke return from London far outweighed the expected run of a two or three weeks in the Pike, at a bus-fare salary in a production I assumed would attract only the cognoscenti. How wrong I was. *Godot* was a sensation and ran for months.

I saw the show from out front, and for the first twenty minutes sat bemused. What was the storyline? Where was the plot? Then some grain of intelligence took root, counselling me to cast aside conventional expectations of a beginning, middle and end, and concentrate on what was unfolding. Which I did, but it would be presumptuous to pretend that by the final curtain I knew I had witnessed what was to become a classic of modern theatre, that I had experienced something new and immensely stimulating. Since then I have seen the play many times and have enjoyed each viewing, especially those productions that do not treat the script with the solemnity of Holy Writ, but allow its essential music hall element to infuse the action.

All of which leads indirectly to An Tóstal, launched in 1953. The Official Souvenir Programme outlined 'A programme of cultural, social and sporting events designed to express the Irish way of life and revive the spirit which animated the traditional Gaelic Festival for which Ireland was famous when Europe was young.' The Irish abroad were encouraged to return home for a visit, and a welcoming hand was extended to strangers. Throughout the country there was open air singing and dancing in traditional costume. There was currach racing in the West and, for all I know, tug-o-warring on the village green. Dublin hung out flags, and erected the Bowl of Light on O'Connell

Bridge, a structure of flowerbeds, the centrepiece a bowl of plastic flames. Its tenure was brief. Myles na gCopaleen dubbed it 'The Tomb of the Unknown Gurrier', and some frolicsome youths (Trinity students, it was suspected) cast it into The Liffey, whether from high spirits or as a gesture to good taste is uncertain.

The Pageant of Cuchulainn was presented in Croke Park. Hilton Edwards directed. With his usual flourish, brandishing a loud-hailer, he rode on horseback during one rehearsal, and when the noise of overflying aeroplanes interrupted proceedings, he instructed an assistant to ring the airport and have flights cancelled while he was rehearsing. These colourful gestures dropped the jaws of the assembled schools, choirs and confraternities press-ganged into service as throngs mustering at Tara, and armies slogging it out with sword and shield. Old hands, accustomed to the flamboyance of Edwards and Mac Liammóir, merely smiled.

Ray McAnally played the mythic hero, but whether I played serf or chieftain, I cannot recall. It was the first of three pageants in Croke Park with which I was connected. The third was *Aiseirigh*, in which I was assistant director to Tomás Mac Anna in 1966, the fiftieth anniversary of the 1916 Rising. Between came *The Pageant of Saint Patrick*, directed by Michael O'Herlihy. Anew McMaster played the saint, reviving a performance he had previously given on the Hill of Slane. Garbed in magnificent red, I played the evil druid, Bricriu, which, added to my performance in *Cuchulainn*, allows me to surprise my sporting friends by declaring that I twice played in Croke Park.

An Tóstal did not survive for more than a few years, but from it evolved the Dublin Theatre Festival, inaugurated by Brendan Smith in 1957. This was the year of *The Rose Tattoo*, remembered by those

of us who were around at the time for the outrageous act of censorship that landed Alan Simpson, the director, in jail.

It was the era of censorship. Publications were banned by the score.
Joyce topped the list, followed by Shaw, Frank O'Connor, Patrick
Kavanagh, Kate O'Brien and Liam O'Flaherty, names to decorate the
canon not only of Irish but of international literature. The slightest
hint of anything deemed to be depraved came under the scrutiny of
the clerical and lay guardians of the nation's morals. Censorship
Boards and Leagues of Decency abounded. Behind them was the
Catholic Church, zealous to protect the morality of its congregation
as part of a wider plan to exclude 'foreign influences' from infiltrating
the defensive cordon of its control. Contraceptives rated high on the
taboo list of church and state. During the action of *The Rose Tattoo*, a
contraceptive is suggested to Seraphina, the leading character, before
being angrily rejected. The prop is hardly seen. The business was so
well performed by Anna Manahan and Pat Nolan, the players
involved, that the audience believed a contraceptive had been on view.
In fact there was no prop. It was all mime.

My tenuous connection with the case was to have stood outside
the Pike with distinguished protesters, including Brendan Behan and
Donagh MacDonagh, while, within, Gardaí observed the play from
the wings, notebooks at the ready to detail any orgy that might occur.
On appeal, the case was thrown out of court, proving that all our
national authorities were not provincially censorious. Since then no
such charge has been brought against any theatre performance, bearing out the observation of Mrs Patrick Campbell, leading West End
actress and contemporary of George Bernard Shaw, that 'it's all right

so long as you don't do it in public and frighten the horses.' We no longer have horses on our streets.

In later years, for Gemini, I directed a revue called *A Keane Sense of Humour*, constructed from the humorous writing of John B. Keane. One of the sketches was based on the mix-up in a small town when a box of contraceptives, intended for a local lady, and a box of Rosary Beads, intended for the parish priest, cross in the post. Playing the puzzled priest, Martin Dempsey, in an effort to work out the purpose of these mysterious items, opened a packet and unrolled one on to his finger. Hilarious laughter. Not a moral guardian leaping to his or her feet in protest. And this hardly a generation after the uproar about *The Rose Tattoo*.

Looking back over the years there seems to have been something of the circus about *The Rose Tattoo* affair, but it was no joke at the time, least of all for Alan Simpson, arrested as a 'purveyor of indecent and obscene material'. The circumstance is fascinatingly documented in *Spyked*, written by the late Carolyn Swift and Gerald Whelan. They conclude that Archbishop John Charles McQuaid was not, as was generally presumed, the direct perpetrator of the incident, even if his shadow fell across it. But there was no doubt about his direct involvement the following year when Sean O'Casey offered *The Drums of Father Ned* to the Theatre Festival. Also on the programme were *Bloomsday*, an adaptation by Allan McClelland of Joyce's *Ulysses*, and three mime plays by Samuel Beckett.

The O'Casey play opens with the Black and Tans destroying a small town. Two prominent citizens are taken prisoner and condemned to execution. The pair have opposing political views and, even when facing the firing squad, refuse to shake hands. Upon which the British officer in charge stops the execution, claiming that 'They will do far more damage to Ireland alive than dead.' The action moves on to the launch of a *tóstal* in the same town. Still in control are the same two men, still at odds, still unable to agree. The political symbolism was obvious. It was even more obvious when the Civil War was still fodder for the hustings and IRA campaigns were common. More than that, O'Casey had publicly supported Alan Simpson during *The Rose Tattoo* affair and was an acknowledged Communist sympathiser.

Archbishop McQuaid had said a mass to inaugurate the 1957 festival, and the dust of *The Rose Tattoo* had not yet settled when he was asked to say a mass to open the 1958 festival. He enquired if plays by O'Casey and Joyce were to be included. Informed that they were, he declined.

Consternation. Fraught meetings.

The Dublin Theatre Festival operated under the auspices of An Tóstal, sponsored by Bord Fáilte. Had only one or two individuals been involved, perhaps a stand would have been taken against the Archbishop – on reflection, perhaps not – but committees are committees and, apart from 'protecting the good name of Ireland', financial interests were involved.

Alterations to the script were requested. O'Casey refused and withdrew the play. Later he would claim that the play was banned. Not so – not according to the letter of the law – but if one is not to underestimate the power of the Archbishop's disapproval, it certainly was. The other play under fire was *Bloomsday*. This, also, was dropped from the programme, and in sympathy Beckett withdrew his mime plays. Thus three major names in the firmament of Irish writing were dropped from the programme of a national theatre festival, which must be a record of some sort. The festival was postponed, then cancelled.

Nowadays it is easy to say 'So what?' if an Archbishop refuses to say an inaugural mass. But today is not yesterday. Today, no one would bother to ask a parish priest, let alone an Archbishop, to say a mass to inaugurate a sports day, or anything else. But in the fifties the shadow cast by a bishop was long, that cast by Archbishop John Charles McQuaid immeasurable. His all-seeing eye scrutinised every activity from parish hall jumble sale to diocesan celebration. From high and low, informants dropped memos on his Drumcondra desk, and the government itself was far from independent of his episcopal influence.

Some years after its rejection by the Dublin Theatre Festival, *Bloomsday* came my way when John Ryan asked me to direct it in the Eblana. For reasons other than artistic, it was an unforgettable production.

The stage of the Eblana was roughly triangular, designed to accommodate a cinema screen, not theatrical sets. Wing space was minimal. Two dressing rooms were packing-case size, each capable of accommodating two in comfort, three or four under pressure if the actors stood. When the cast was large, the dressing rooms were utilised in relays, like bunks in a doss house. *Bloomsday* was staged with a cast of twenty-five or so, the players making-up in relays in the tiny dressing rooms, on the stage before the doors opened, and after curtain-up on the steps that led down to the theatre entrance. Latecomers had the unusual experience of stepping over make-up boxes, discarded street clothes, and half-naked citizens of Joyce's Dublin.

A couple of weeks before rehearsal was due to commence, John Ryan despatched me to London to discuss the script with Allan McClelland. On landing, I rang for directions to his home. He wanted to know what I was drinking.

'Gin.'

A bottle was waiting when I stepped from the taxi.

Allan claimed that he was not drinking, but he kept my gin company with a few beers and a bottle or so of wine. *Bloomsday* was not discussed. 'Enjoy yourself,' was his answer when I brought up the subject. 'We can work tomorrow.'

Tomorrow I was in that state of jerky energy induced by too little sleep and gin souring into a thudding hangover. By coincidence, Allan was rehearsing a version of *Ulysses* in the BBC. He insisted that I accompany him to rehearsal, and we were driven there in a Mini owned by a young woman who was a member of the cast. Her car was three inches deep in newspapers and her face deathly pale, a result, Allan explained, of the shock she had suffered when her husband walked out. Rounding Hyde Park Corner, over the back of his seat Allan proffered me a half-tumbler of brandy while the Mini dodged about among towering double-deckers. Life was leaning towards the surreal.

At lunchtime I hung on to reality while Allan managed half a bottle of wine and a couple of beers. By now, far from deploring his drinking, I was astounded at his ability to function normally, which I was not. When the evening brought out the bottles again, I was racked with guilt. I had come to London to work and here I was desperately trying to keep pace with an alcoholic in full flight. I tried to squeeze in a few words about *Bloomsday* but they were drowned in liquor.

Next morning I was fragile glass threatening to splinter. Allan was washed, shaved and ready for the day. Seeing me into a taxi, he said, 'Those additions you asked for last night' – I could barely remember last night – 'you'll have them in a couple of days.' And I did.

The play was allotted two weeks' rehearsal, little enough time for a straightforward piece but testing for a script with a huge cast and a kaleidoscope of short scenes. Ronnie Walsh was cast as Bloom – a part he would repeat memorably in Micheál Ó'hAodha's day-long version of *Bloomsday* produced by Radio Éireann. But this was not radio. This was the stage, and Bloom was in every scene. Ronnie was a fine actor but he had problems, one of them a casual approach to learning lines, another an addiction to the gee-gees. Where the race meeting was, there too was Ronnie.

Four days into rehearsal, he vanished. Not a sign of him all day. Nor the next. Nor the following. When I appealed to John Ryan – I may even have demanded that Ronnie be replaced – he replied with an airy, 'Oh, he'll be back', and left it to us. 'There's a pair of them in it,' said a thunderous Anna Manahan.

Rehearsals staggered on. Stand-ins read Ronnie's lines and a glowering Anna performed in a vacuum. I prayed – in extremis there is nothing left but prayer – and God answered. Someone answered. Something answered. Something clicked.

Where do ideas come from? One moment we are lost in thickets of confusion, the next we see a way through the forest. Wherever it came from, an idea surfaced and I held my breath waiting to try it out when Ronnie returned, if he ever did. 'Oh he will,' volunteered a head buried in the racing page of the *Indo*, 'Cheltenham' – or Newmarket or wherever – 'finishes today and he'll be back.' And so he was, head bowed like a guilty schoolboy when I had a go at him. Not that I delivered my lecture with any hope of reforming Ronnie, but I had to put on a show before the icy presence of the leading lady fuming in the background.

Rehearsal proceeded. I put my bright idea into operation. It was very simple: at the end of each scene, instead of asking Ronnie to move, I instructed him to remain centre stage and let the next scene, actors and furnishings, form around him. It worked. It worked so well that it even looked as if I had planned it from the beginning.

Allan arrived for the dress rehearsal, primed and ready for action. At his side was his secretary, a mature lady of quiet refinement, in her hand a pencil and notepad, in her handbag a bottle and glass. Throughout the rehearsal Allan dictated, at first in a whisper but as the evening progressed with rising audibility. Not only could I hear him from my position in the fourth row, so too could the actors onstage. Not that every comment was critical – 'Excellent, Ronnie' and 'Very good, Anna' was stage-whispered around the small theatre. But with the emptying of the bottle came a mood change. 'Ridiculous,' was heard. 'Bloody awful.' And even louder, 'That's not the fucking line. Make a note of it. Yes, exactly as I said. I'll spell it for you – F.U.C.K.I.N.G.'

By now it was near the interval and I decided that in the break I would give Allan the choice of keeping quiet or of getting out. But I was forestalled. A voice from the stage, a voice not to be trifled with, shouted angrily, 'Shut up Allan, for Christ's sake, and let us get on with it up here.' It was Ronnie. He'd had enough. I expected a show-down but Allan took it like a lamb, and when the interval arrived, instead of sulking, he said how splendid everything and everyone was.

Even then, *Bloomsday* did not sail in untroubled waters. Never known for memorising accurately, Ronnie gave a casual rendering of his lines. In the final scene we are left with three characters, Jim Norton as Stephen and Ronnie as Bloom on stage level, Anna as Molly upstairs in bed. There is no direct interplay between them, each is locked in private thoughts, each delivers a speech, then gives way to one of the others. Simple, one would think, but not with Ronnie ambling from one speech to another, inventing and ad-libbing. It was not that he could not improvise – at that he was a master – but the only cue he gave was to stop speaking and let someone else get on with it. Conversely, when one of the others paused, he was quite likely to butt in.

Anna Manahan was an actress of great precision. Not unreasonably she expected clear-cut cues and no interruption during a dramatic pause. She also has a well-trained voice. When Ronnie interrupted one of her pauses, the result was a vocal Howitzer silencing a cap gun. When he gave a wrong cue, or none, a seething Molly rocked in bed with more than sexual passion. I have seen many actresses play Molly's soliloquy but never one who delivered the final 'yes … yes … yes …' with more palpable relief.

Bloomsday was a success, and after the festival it was revived and transferred to the Gate. Allan returned to see it, not drinking now, genuinely not drinking. He was a changed man. Everything he had been enthusiastic about in the Eblana he bitched in the Gate, coldly and contemptuously. I listened with tight lips and tried to console myself by attributing his about-face to withdrawal symptoms.

Ronnie was a fine actor, with distinguished work in the Abbey and in radio behind him, but unreliability took its toll and work no longer came his way, though not before I directed him and Aiden Grennell in a production of Pinter's *No Man's Land* in the now defunct Oscar Theatre in Ballsbridge. It was Ronnie's production. He knew his lines and gave a fine performance. That was my last theatrical contact with him, although whenever we met he told me he had a project in mind and would give me a ring. Regrettably – not that I expected it – he never did.

Throughout these years I saw little of my parents; a few days here, a few days there, and ever thoughts of getting back to the next job in Dublin. My mother's sight, which had begun to fail when we lived in Monaghan, was now reduced to shadows. Her life had not been easy. It was she who bore the brunt of my father's imbalance, who shielded her children, whose defence was impenetrable silence, a refusal to speak, to argue, to remonstrate, a silence that drove him deeper into the flailing hopelessness that beset him.

I was a late child, perhaps an unexpected one, eight years younger than the youngest of my sisters, now long left home, Vera to nurse in England, Toni to work in the telephone exchange of a southern town, and Maureen, the eldest, to marry and live in Balbriggan. When I was a boy, it had been my joy to walk with my mother after school, long walks in sunshine or in rain. We spoke little; companionship was all. When her sight was failing, I prayed diligently that it would be restored, and yet a secret, perverse part of me dwelt on the possibility of being a boy whose mother was blind. Is it usual for children to think in such a manner, or only those with the stirrings of the actor in them that transposes life into an ongoing performance?

In Mullingar, because of her blindness, even though she used a stick for guidance, our days of walking together were ended. In the afternoons I sat with her, at ease as I could never be in my father's company. I played golf with him, and improved my game on the Mullingar course under the tutorship of the local professional, but, if truth be told, when I dropped home it was to see my mother, not my father.

This was the fifties. Life was changing. The breakup with Nora

Lever did not close with a spectacular row, it faded away. Running the company had held us together, but too many disagreements, personal and professional (made worse by the temporary intervention of an attractive English actress) signalled that an end must come. The separation dragged on too long. Such is the way of partings.

I moved to a six-by-ten bedsitter in Leeson Street that masqueraded as a flat. Standing between bed and washbasin, I was monarch of my little reign. By stretching I could touch each wall, but freedom was mine, such as I had not experienced since I arrived in Dublin to join Ria Mooney's school of acting.

Nora and I had already done our last show together when Phyllis Ryan approached me in Groomes Hotel to read a play with a view to directing it. Either Phyllis did not make her meaning immediately clear or I was slow to comprehend – the night was well advanced and the decibels were high – but eventually I gathered that the script she offered me had been rejected by another director and she would not be offended if I turned it down. The author was John B. Keane, the author of *Sive*, a play that hit the headlines when it was launched on the amateur drama circuit the previous year.

I had met John B. when I adjudicated at the All-Ireland Amateur Drama finals in Athlone. 'Met' is hardly correct, I saw him across a smoke- and drink-stoked reception in the Hudson Bay Hotel when *Sive* won the premier award, the Esso Trophy. To join the revelry I climbed through a window in full evening dress. It was that sort of celebration.

Early in that amateur drama season a headline ran that, 'Local Man's Play Wins At Drama Festival.' For a play by a local author to reach a festival stage was unusual but not unknown, but when *Sive* won a second time the press pricked up its ears. It was explained that

142

Sive was a girl's name, the author a John Keane from Listowel, identified as a brother of the actor Eamon Keane, and a publican, someone
was sure to add, as if, in a literary generation not renowned for sobriety, selling liquor was less inspirational than drinking it.

Headlines celebrated the triumphant progress of *Sive* around the
festival circuit. In no time the author's name figured as prominently as
that of his play – *Keane's Sive wins again*, *Premier Trophy for John B.
Keane and Listowel Players*, and so on. *Sive*, it seemed, was unstop-
pable.

Professional theatre thrives on tales of overnight stardom, but who
would have forecast that the few weeks of an amateur drama season
would make household names of *Sive* and John B. Keane? But that's
what happened. John B. and his play became national names and the
public turned its eyes towards the finals in Athlone.

Then, sensation. At the Charleville Festival, *Sive* was beaten. The
wires hummed. Did *Sive* have an off-night? Was it not really as good
as it was hyped? There was charge and counter-charge; accusations of
prejudice on the part of the adjudicator – 'That fella is from the
Abbey and he had it in for Kerry' – and of bad sportsmanship on the
part of the group – 'The Kerry crowd can't take a beating.' All of
which, when latched onto by the press, built up the excitement for the
final.

I was adjudicating at Athlone that year, and, from a lifetime of
theatregoing, I remember no more electricity in the air than on the
night *Sive* took to the boards. The hall was jammed, the box office
besieged. John B. arrived, flanked by kith and kin and a Listowel
mafia that would urge the play on as vigorously as they would urge on
a Kerry football team in Croke Park.

From the first line the play took hold, and by the final curtain I had witnessed the grip that John B. at his best exerts on an audience. The highlight was the arrival of Pats Bocock and the Carthalawn travelling men – 'Tinkers' as we then called them, bearing with them a hint of Greek chorus allied to the power of the poet to celebrate the good man or satirise the villain. Their entry was heralded by the beating of a bodhrán, a sound unfamiliar to many in the audience. At the time, led by the music of Seán Ó Riada and the radio programmes of Ciarán Mac Mathúna, there was a resurgence of interest in traditional Irish music, part of an awakening of confidence in Irish art and culture, and it may not be an exaggeration to claim that the use of the bodhrán in *Sive* played some small part in turning what had for so long been a hidden Ireland into the visible one.

Speaking from the stage after the performance, my fellow adjudicator John Fernald, an established West End director, declared that it had been an evening of theatrical magic. Only sour opponents and rejected authors disagreed.

Winning at Athlone was not the end of the story. It was commonly believed that *Sive* had been rejected by the Abbey, and no sooner had it won at Athlone than a clamour arose for it to be staged by the National Theatre. Why had it been rejected? Promising but not good enough, we were told, melodramatic, out of date. There was, I suspect, another reason. Nowadays the play can be viewed comfortably as a period piece, but in 1959 it was presented as contemporary Ireland and there was an opinion, implied if not voiced, that *Sive* presented the wrong image of an emerging industrial nation. At the time there was little national confidence about things Irish, and a prickly defensiveness feared that rural Irishness on stage might be construed as stage-Irishness, especially if the play reached London. It was pointed out, not without reason, that the Stage Irishman still strutted the

West End in Big House plays in which London stars played the upstairs aristocracy while Irish actors cavorted downstairs as comic relief. Literary merit means little when national touchiness takes upon itself the defence of national honour.

Whatever the reason for the rejection, if rejection it was, the Abbey, under pressure, had to solve the problem of how to stage *Sive* without reversing the artistic judgement of a few months earlier. The solution would have done Machiavelli proud; Listowel Players were invited to present *Sive* in the Abbey when the company was on holiday. Thus the play was staged in the National Theatre, but the National Theatre had not staged it. The show was a sell-out. The voice of the people had prevailed.

It was a year later that Phyllis Ryan handed me the script of *The Highest House on the Mountain*. One reading and I immediately agreed to direct. The vitality of Keane's characters, the colourful dialogue, the strength of the plot and the forthright expression of repressed sex were powerful driving forces. What Keane presented was more than a racy tale of the Irish countryside; he dealt with sex in a way that reminded a prudish nation that under the surface ran powerful currents.

The play ran to packed houses in the Gas Company Theatre in Dun Laoghaire, with Anna Manahan, Martin Dempsey and Pat Nolan in the leading parts. This was the start of a long association with Gemini and the plays of John B. Keane, an association that continued until the early eighties when I directed *The Chastitute* in the Olympia.

A year after *The Highest House* came *No More in Dust*, the romantic adventure of a Kerry supporter up for the match. It also played in Dun Laoghaire, and, like *The Highest House* enjoyed a long, full-house run. It was a lesser play. During rehearsal, alterations were made to the script. Too many for John's taste. Years later, a company manager anxious to include it in a summer season rang me to ask if I had a copy. I had not. I mentioned the matter to John. He dismissed the play darkly as 'a group effort' and that was that. The play is not listed among his works.

John did not attend rehearsals and it was easy to sense that alterations made to a script, not unusual for a new play in rehearsal for a first production, did not always please him. Lines that had been cut sometimes reappeared in the published version.

The Year of the Hiker, produced a year after *No More in Dust*, is the tale of a man who deserted his wife and young family for the call of the roads. Twenty years later he comes home to die. It is a family play, developing the characters through their response to the returned Hiker. Martin Dempsey played the Hiker and Anna Manahan the deserted wife's sister, the last to make peace with the returned vagrant. It drew the comment from a leading critic of the time, Seamus Kelly of the *Irish Times*, that it was a play with an Ibsenesque quality.

I directed the first production in the early sixties and twenty-five years later directed the play again with Ulster actors for a tour of Northern Ireland. Northern dialect was used, and, with the exception of replacing a few localisms here and there, the play lost nothing in the transition. The impact of a play is not necessarily lessened by a change of accent, despite the claim of some that without the authentic patois a play will suffer. O'Casey without a Dublin accent is unsatisfactory to a Dublin audience, but how about O'Casey in New York? Or Miller in Dublin? Accent is a topping, not a vital ingredient.

The script I used in Belfast was the published version which, in a number of instances, differed from the first production. A major change in the first production was the elimination from the last act of the singing of 'Red Sails in the Sunset', considered mawkish and overly sentimental by myself and by the actors. At amateur drama festivals I saw the play many times, and when the song was sung, invariably self-indulgently, I felt that the decision to cut it in the first production was correct. In Northern Ireland – out of curiosity, but prepared to take action – I left it to the actors. They asked no questions. When the moment came, John Hewitt, Stella McCusker and Trudy Kelly held hands and sang 'Red Sails' with such intensity that the scene was deeply moving, not mawkish as I had feared. There is a moral there somewhere.

These were good years. I was fortunate enough to the direct some of the most successful plays by the most successful writer of the day, John B. Keane. I was rarely out of work. I was confident, and confidence walks with a firm step. But I was in my late thirties and aware that there was more to life than the theatre.

I had lived in digs, bedsitters, attics, basements, holes in the wall, under dripping eaves, in the city centre wakened by clanking morning trams, or too far out for the last bus home. I had lived in a tall thin room, sliced from the gracious expanse of a Georgian sitting room, where the muffled grunts and squeals of a Diarmuid and his panting Gráinne penetrated the paper-thin dividing wall to disturb my solitary bachelordom. I was weary of pub companionship and the transient consolation of eyes across a crowded room. When my parents moved to Balbriggan I was pleased to join them, thinking it would be only for a little time, in no way suspecting that there I would marry and make a permanent home.

When he retired, my father bought a square white bungalow on the outskirts of Youghal. Why he choose Youghal I have no idea.

Perhaps because it was close to my mother's relations in Cork, or perhaps after a lifetime of moving it seemed as good a place as any to find rest. My visits were brief, an occasional few days between engagements, and one long summer holiday when I delighted my father by winning a cup at the local golf course (he had lost by a single shot the previous year).

For a time Youghal suited well. My father enjoyed the high, windblown golf course that overlooked the sea, and was proud of the strawberries he grew against the sunny southern wall. New on the sitting room mantelpiece was a statue of Saint Martin de Porres, a parting gift from a friend in Mullingar. My mother was never comfortable with it. 'Imagine,' she said, 'a black man who is a saint.'

The harsh winter winds of Youghal were unkind to my mother's health and within a few years my parents moved again, this time to Balbriggan, where my sister Maureen was married. It was my mother's last move. Gradually her health declined, her heart weakened and, to avoid the strain of mounting the stairs, her bed was moved down to the sitting room. She lay propped on pillows, her Rosary looped around her fingers. In the morning she felt for her glasses and turned her almost sightless eyes towards the light of the window, as do those who are old and ill and grateful to greet another dawn. The room where she lay was a sombre place. I knew, all her family knew, that she would never leave her bed, but when I said goodbye one morning I did not suspect that she would die before I returned.

My sister Toni was waiting for me. 'I went in to see her. I thought she was asleep but she was unconscious. The doctor could do nothing. I called the others and we were around the bed when she slipped away.'

At my mother's bedside were my sister Maureen and her husband,

Willie, waiting to continue the prayers my arrival had interrupted. I joined the prayers but I did not look on my mother's face.

'How is he?' I asked, meaning my father.

'In bed. Time enough to tell him in the morning.'

I slept little. Nor did my sister. We stayed alert lest my father wake and come downstairs, as he often did, for a cup of tea, never passing my mother's door without opening it. In time I came to understand his need for the reassurance of my mother's presence. She was the pivot of his life and, for all his turbulence, I do not doubt he loved her. So I stayed awake, knowing that there would be no greater cruelty than to allow him to enter her room and, without warning, discover she had died. But he slept on.

Next morning Toni and I were early in the kitchen waiting to hear him on the stairs. When we did, we went into the hall to intercept him. He wore a woollen vest, his braces hung loose about his waist, his feet bare. Before we had time to speak he said, 'I know she's gone.'

For a time he sat on the stairs, his head in his hands, lamenting. When he recovered we helped him back to bed. All morning he lay there. When I knocked and asked if he would like a cup of tea, he turned away and did not answer. Late in the afternoon I heard him on the stairs and would have gone to him but Toni raised a hand. 'Leave him,' she said, instinct telling her that he was entering my mother's room to say goodbye.

I was, mostly, unacquainted with death. On a summer's day, walking on the beach at Balbriggan, I was the first to see the body of a woman floating near the tide line. I helped to drag her from the sea and lay her on the sand, where she rested, heavy and motionless, water pouring from her mouth. The experience was impersonal, no more than the chance witnessing of the drowning of an unknown woman.

Now death had come within the doors of my family, and I feared to enter my mother's room and look upon it. But I must. It was my duty.

Forcing myself, I went in and sat by her bed, where I had so often sat to keep her company when she was alive. But I did not look upon her face. I said a prayer and rose to go. Since her death, throughout the night listening for movement in my father's room, in the morning pinning crepe to the door and greeting sympathisers, I had not grieved, and could not understand why I was unmoved. But to leave so coldly would be to fail her. And myself.

Bracing myself, I turned to the bed and looked upon her, and with that look I found the courage to kiss her brow, and in the instant my lips touched her forehead I was freed of dread. It was no lifeless thing I kissed, it was my mother. And having kissed her I could grieve, and grieving, sit in peace with her and with her death.

After death a person lives on in the memories of others. Of all the memories I have of my mother, none is so vivid as that moment of kissing her goodbye. I see her calm and in repose. It is my most cherished memory of her.

A year after my mother's death I married Nancy McCullen. She was a farmer. This I must repeat when I speak of her to those who did not know her, city folk and town dwellers.

'My wife is a farmer.'

A sceptical pause.

'She's a farmer.'

An eyebrow raised.

'She drives tractors. She reaps. She sows. She de-horns cattle. She docks lamb's tails. She midwifes ewes during the lambing season.

She sits at a desk and does the paperwork, but that she finds boring.'

End of conversation.

The name of Nancy's farm is Salmon. It lies on rolling land in Fingal, north County Dublin. Our bedroom window looked out on growing crops, on harvests, on frost, on beasts, pheasants, hares, a wheeling buzzard, a hovering kestrel, a fox, once on a scampering mink, on tractors, balers, a plough, potato harvesters, the machinery that sows, reaps, and sows again, a mix of life unknown to the itinerant urban ways of my father's job or the enclosed nature of the theatre.

Nancy was the eldest of three sisters. After leaving school she assisted her father in running the farm, particularly in the years of his decline. On his death it was her inheritance. Had there been a boy in the family the farm would have been his, and what of Nancy then? The academic world would have attracted that hint of her Aunt Mary I saw in her, Aunt Mary who could enumerate the seed breed and generation of every Big House family and holding in Meath, north County Dublin and places farther flung. In her declining years, Nancy and I visited her in the Lourdes Hospital in Drogheda, where she was more resident than patient.

Visiting was a lesson in lineage. Leaving was a problem. On a day when time was short, we decided to pay our brief respects and go, but no sooner had we arrived than Mary launched into the history of some past landlord family, and by the time we had inched backwards to the bedroom door we were through four generations of births, marriages and deaths. Which was no more than a preamble, because Mary accompanied us to the main entrance, spreading the net wider to include inheritances, illegitimacies, and squandered fortunes. If ever a natural academic was undirected, a gifted researcher lost, it was Aunt Mary. She did not marry. She read avidly and kept house eccentrically. It is said that on an occasion when visitors arrived she was despatched to make tea, and when she had not returned an hour later was found buried in a yellowed newspaper that lined a press. There was something of Aunt Mary in Nancy, not the part that went to make tea and forgot to come back – Nancy was a meticulous hostess, ever welcoming, ever attentive. It was the student in her that reminded me of Mary; head in a book when television blared, her keen examination, guidebook in hand, of ancient sites and ruins. Her judgement on drama I learned to value and be slow to question. She saw the text where I saw the acting and the sets.

We met at the golf club in Balbriggan, casually as people do who nod to one another on fairways, or exchange an offhand 'Hello' in the clubhouse. My comings and goings to visit my parents were irregular and it was some time before I got to know her well. At a party in Dublin some time into the new year of 1961, and not enjoying it, I remembered that there was a gathering that evening in the golf club in Balbriggan and that Nancy was likely to be there. I took a bus and found her. In May we were married.

From the beginning, perhaps from the moment I decided to leave the party for Balbriggan, I had no doubt that I wanted to marry Nancy. I had never before wanted to marry. There had been romantic entanglements and brief encounters that faded with the sunrise, but nothing that endured. My youth, bred on novelettish Victorian romanticism, rejected the base thought that what I called love might be no more than the restless drive of sex. Love was elevated. Love was the tiled aisle to the altar rails. Sex was base. Sex was the roving eye enslaved by silk stockings and a shapely blouse. That it takes two to tango didn't enter into it.

On Saint Patrick's Days, particularly if the weather is bitterly cold,

I recall that on such a day Nancy came to visit me when I was adjudicating in Bundoran. Separate rooms, as she would have expected, and I too. It was in Bundoran that I proposed, and I can still see her thoughtful look before she answered, 'I do not want to live the rest of my life without you.' That thoughtful look would become familiar to me. She made no hurried decisions.

We were married in Balbriggan. I would have settled for a quiet wedding but that was not Nancy's way. Family, meaning aunts, uncles and cousins numberless, must partake of her celebration. My contribution was my family and a few close friends. Offering age as an excuse, my father did not attend. Perhaps he thought that his absence would attract more attention than his presence, or perhaps I shift unjustly to him my own uncertainties. Upbringing festers in the gut. Home background shapes the individual. Once out the door to independence the youth believes he can shake free, but childhood clings, the ghost of insecurity still haunts.

Nancy's decision to marry me could not have been lightly reached. To bring an actor into the world of farming must have raised many a neighbouring eyebrow. Farming and the theatre, how could it last? Had her father, God rest him, been alive, what would he have thought? But she proceeded with the dignity of one assured of her place in life, and I was the recipient of a love that would sustain me through all the years until her death. And afterwards.

Our honeymoon night was spent in the Old Ground Hotel in Ennis. When I walk the streets of that town I am reminded of that beginning, the beginning of all that would endure. From the Old Ground we moved to Parknasilla, where we went boating on a day of searing sunshine, the sky transparent, the water a burning glass to tan the skin. Leaving our bedroom, I threw a newspaper on the dressing table, a photograph of our wedding on an open page. Spotting it, Nancy folded the paper and put it in a waste paper basket. Attention-seeking she deplored. Her life was too important for such triviality.

Next to Killarney. We played golf and walked in the evening where rutting rams head-butted in contest for in-season ewes, the collision of heads echoing brutally in the surrounding trees while a placid sun reflected from a placid lake.

I ran out of cash. Carelessness. Until then I had never bothered with a chequebook and had stupidly underestimated how much cash I would need. Not that I worried. Nancy would have her chequebook. But she did not. She had left it at home.

In the area lived a friend. I rang, inviting him and his wife to Killarney for a drink. He was a man of highly developed instinct. Without prompting he beckoned me to follow him to the toilet. 'How much do you need?'

'Remember, this is a loan.'

'Call it a wedding present.'

A decent man, John B.

Nancy thought to instruct me in farming. I was a poor student. Holding a gate open while stock were herded into a yard, or driving a tractor to deliver fodder during the winter months was the pinnacle of my farming skills. When the ground was iron hard and grass was rimed with frost there was a unique invigoration in the clear icy air of a winter's day. Looking seawards from the highest point of Salmon, I could see the coast all the way from the Mourne Mountains to the Sugar Loaf, and never took for granted how fortunate I was to have a life far removed from rehearsal rooms and dusty stages. Which reminds me of a visit to Salmon by the actor Norman Rodway. It was around Christmas, the ground rock-hard, the ditches iced over. After a walk around the land, I expected him to comment on the beauty of the landscape or the joys of country living, but his only comment was that never in his life had he seen so much frozen shite.

The lambing season was the time when last-gasp lambs lay in cardboard boxes at the open door of the Aga, or under the infrared lamp in a small shed known as the intensive care unit. Few weaklings survived, but Nancy did not give up easily. Her acid test was to put the patient on its feet. If it could stand, even shakily, there was hope. If it collapsed, more heat was applied. Abandonment was not in her nature. I once told her that when my time came I would prefer if she did not hoist me to my feet but left things to the medics. She was not amused.

When a ewe was in difficulties delivering a lamb, my contribution was to hold a lamp when Nancy rolled up her sleeves, often of her dressing gown, and went down on her knees in the squelching straw to midwife a delivery. On the way home from a reception we were driving up the New Lane when, in the headlights, we spotted the bobbing, luminous eyes of a flock of sheep that had broken out from Salmon. We were in evening dress. Rain was falling and the field into which the sheep turned was deep in mud. I would have gone to Salmon for Wellingtons but Nancy did not hesitate. Grabbing a flashlamp, she was out of the car, her evening dress tucked into her knickers, and off through the mud and briars to round-up the fleeing herd.

To engage my farming inclinations, she suggested pigs. We dealt with a man who had a shed-full of Bonhams – rather, Nancy did the dealing while I contemplated my squealing fortune. Some who learned of the enterprise wondered how I could bear to feed animals and then ferry them to the abattoir. In answer I told a story of the actor Ronnie Walsh, who at one time owned a farm and a herd of Friesian cattle. Faced with a sentimentalist who wondered how he could rear animals then send them for slaughter, his answer was curt, 'They're not fucking pets, you know.'

A visiting friend, Paddy Bolger of *The Farmers Journal* (my connection was amateur drama not animal welfare), cast a brief eye on the shed where the pigs were housed and forecast that, with open windows and cold air rushing in, there was little chance of the pigs fattening. He was right. But once committed, I persevered.

Then came disaster. Carrying feed to a trough I slipped and sprained my ankle, and for two weeks was confined to the sitting room sofa. Word of this mishap reached the world of amateur drama, where I was known as an adjudicator. A friend from a provincial town rang to tell me of the wild rumour that claimed I had slipped in a pig-house and sprained my ankle. How could such a misfortune, he wondered, befall one of my sophistication who, like Cecily in *The Importance of Being Earnest*, had never seen a spade, let alone a pig? When I confirmed the story the only sympathy I got was a bellow of laughter. He probably dined out on the story for weeks.

When the pigs were fit they were loaded into a trailer and brought to the factory. In due course a cheque arrived and the profit calculated. The pigs had barely broken even. Never again did a pig cross the threshold of Salmon.

When my mother died my father did not attend the removal of her coffin to the church, or the funeral next day. 'You understand why?' he begged. 'Yes,' I said. He was in pain and it was no time to disagree.

Next morning he said, 'Another one gone.' I assumed that he was speaking of my mother, but he continued. 'In Ballyneal or somewhere.'

I collected the newspaper when it was pushed through the letter box and handed it to him. He turned at once to the Deaths column and pointed to an entry. 'He'd have been a second or third cousin.'

It is easy now to identify the depression that disturbed my father, but it was then unfashionable to believe the mind to be as vulnerable as the body. Mental problems were attributed to weakness of will, those who suffered were exhorted to 'pull themselves together'. The hurt my father caused to others was plain to see, that he suffered great personal distress won no sympathy.

Maturity had not taught me how to overcome the guarded reticence with which I approached him, and which I was resigned to think would forever hang like an albatross about our relationship. Yet there were moments I cherished. On one Sunday evening I was waiting for a broadcast of *The Well of the Saints*. The radio was in the sitting room where he was reading. 'Do you mind if I switch it on?'

He nodded and went on reading. Shortly after the play began he put the paper aside and closed his eyes. I thought he had fallen asleep but he was listening intently. When the broadcast ended he asked who wrote it.

'John M. Synge.'

'Synge,' he repeated, seeming to explore the name for what it was that stirred him. 'I could see the country people and the roads where I was born,' he said, and remained with his eyes closed, revisiting a time long past.

When he could no longer live alone, my eldest sister Maureen made over a room in her house and he moved in. At first, the centre of attention, he was an affable grandparent who amused the children, but the old destroyer was not dead, and in time his inescapable, sad story was repeated. He spread destruction and blamed it on others. He pined in his room, which soon became a fortress bristling with self-pity and imagined slights.

It is sad to turn a cold face towards an ageing parent, but knowing my father's febrile disposition, and that his lifelong destructiveness would not alter, I determined that under no circumstances would I invite him to live in Salmon. It was not without regret that I reached such a decision, but my first duty was to Nancy and a growing family, and, as surely as night follows day, I knew that if my father came to live in Salmon he would inevitably cause the same friction and distress that Maureen suffered. How long she could have borne it I do not know, but without warning he decided to visit his niece and nephews who lived on the outskirts of New Ross, close to his birthplace of Ballyneal. He set a date, and I drove him to Dublin to catch a train to the south-east. When he bought a single ticket I was surprised. Two weeks later I understood why. In a letter he explained that he had consulted a doctor who booked him into a home for retired people. It was run by nuns and very peaceful. He was in good hands and I was not to worry. His nephew, Jim, would look after him and he would stay for as long as the doctor thought advisable. Halfway through the letter I realised that he had planned it all. He had deserted his family.

The Haughton Hospital in New Ross was where he settled, and it was there I had final evidence of his gift for sensing death in his family. Phil, his favourite brother, was long emigrated to America, but a couple of times in the fifties he and his wife, Jeanette, paid a visit back home. When they reached Dublin, Phil was always in form for a late-night Guinness in Groomes Hotel. Walking back to his hotel on one such visit I turned down a back alley. Phil hesitated. 'It's OK,'

I said. 'This is Dublin, not Chicago.' But his hand slid into his jacket pocket. 'I always carry one,' he said.

In the Roaring Twenties Phil was a cop in Chicago. Jocularly, I asked if he knew Al Capone.

'Sure. Everyone knew Al.'

'What was he like?'

Phil smiled, 'You treat Al right and Al treated you right.' Enough said.

When Phil died, rather than get in touch with my father directly and upset him with the news, Jeanette contacted my cousin, Jim, who lived in New Ross. 'I sat by his bed,' Jim said. 'I told him I had some bad news, but before I could say any more he reached for his diary.' 'I know what your news is,' he said, pointing to an entry opposite the date of Phil's death. 'Phil died. Knock 5.30 am,' reminding me of Monaghan days when he foretold the death of a relation with the 'rap rap-rap' he called the Knock.

I did not question Jim's story. I did not question my father's fore-knowledge. I have the diary still.

Shortly after he moved into the home I found him sitting in the sun, sprucely dressed as ever in a three-piece suit and knotted tie. He was now in his eighties, stooped a little, leaning on his stick, the same stick he had swung fashionably when he was younger and stepped it out army style. He was happy in the home, he told me. Jim kept an eye on him and he was fed like a gamecock. Laughing, he said, 'I know I can be troublesome sometimes, boy. I was so long in charge in the Post Office I forget I am in charge no longer.'

Ominous words, I thought, and I was right. The gloss wore off and soon, on my way to visit him, I would try to think of possible topics of conversation. Nothing made much difference, he was ever complaining, ever dejected. In time, the inevitable happened. The Matron phoned. Was I coming to visit my father?

'Is he unwell?'

'His health is good. He is a very strong man. But I don't think we can keep him here much longer.'

I went straight to New Ross. The Matron interviewed me in her office. 'He snaps at the nurses. He stays in bed. He won't eat his meals.'

'How long has this been going on?'

'Some weeks this time. But since he came, he's had bouts. We do our best but nothing satisfies him.'

'I don't think his problem is physical.'

'Possibly not. But he seems unwilling or incapable of doing anything to help himself, and there is no specialist here to attend him.'

When I knocked on his door there was no answer. I went in. He was in bed, his face turned from the light. A newspaper was scattered on the floor, a cup of tea had gone cold on the bedside locker. The window was closed and the distinctive odour of infirmity was sprinkled in the half-light of the drawn curtains.

When he recognised me he wept. I turned to open the curtains, but he called, 'Don't. I can't bear it.' He was awash with grief. I tried to comfort him but he would not be comforted. In childhood, echoed now in the tension of this darkened room, Mother would have tightened her lips and I, her ally, would have taken her side. But the years, and something of my father in myself, had given me some insight into the depression from which he suffered, and I was less quick to censure.

Words oozed like puss from his anguish. 'No one talks to me. Better if I was dead and gone. Better for all of you. Sometimes I shout but it's no good.'

All I could offer was a presence to absorb his pain.

'They won't talk to me. They won't listen. A bitch that one. Standing in the door telling me off. She forgets I ran one of the biggest post offices in the country. What the hell would she know, stuck in a convent all her life?' In bewilderment he stared at the wall. 'I don't want to be like this. Something happens to me. I'm tired of being like this.'

When he was calm I opened the curtains and let in the light. 'I'll find you somewhere else. Near Dublin. Near me.'

At parting, when I prepared to say goodbye, he gestured towards the wardrobe. 'My attaché case.'

I was the same case he had carried with him when he went on his rounds to check sub-post offices in his district, the same broken lock, the same strap around it to keep it secure. 'Take it. There are things in it I want you to have.'

On the way home I pulled to the side of the road and opened the case. In it were his war medals, his army issue watch, a photograph of a winning Kilkenny hurling team, a youthful portrait taken on the day he entered the post office, and a snapshot taken on the bridge at Killaloe when I was still in short trousers, my mother on one side, he on the other. There were postcards to my mother, his 'Dearest Girl,' despatched from France after the Armistice of 1918. There was a bayonet sheathed in its scabbard, a German infantryman's uniform cap, an invitation to my sister Maureen's wedding, and a copy of my mother's death notice. And, probing forgotten corners of my memory and shaking emotion from the dust, I found a child's drawing of a racing car, a broken ruler with half my name on it, and a misspelt postcard I had written from a Boy Scout camp. But what struck deepest was finding, still in the envelope in which it was despatched, the university report from Cork that I had failed my Pre-Medical examination. He had kept it all these years. He had preserved his disappointment side by side with press notices that mentioned my name.

Before returning the items to the case, I looked over the countryside where I was parked, his native Kilkenny that he loved and in his heart had never left. He had handed me his life and the part I played in it. And how I wished I could have responded to his love.

5

Throughout the sixties and seventies the atmosphere of a Keane first night was unique. The chatter of Dublin was drowned by the resonance of Kerry. Kerry speaks loudly. Kerry speaks confidently. Not for nothing is Kerry known as The Kingdom. The Olympia on a Keane first night was a lesser Croke Park, with Kerry going for four-in-a-row.

An acquaintance, an unfulfilled writer, claimed that the plays of Keane lacked construction and wallowed in sentiment, not to mention the misguided audiences who lauded the author. 'Kerry is a state of mind' was his chant. Of course Kerry is a state of mind. So is being a Dub or a Corkonian or a Belfast man. The Liffey, the Lee and the Lagan are contrasting stimuli for the imagination. Who wants uniformity?

I had an immediate affinity with the plays of John B. We are from similar backgrounds, small-townies with strong rural connections, and of more or less the same age. His characters inhabited my father's home in south Kilkenny, they lived only a couple of fields distant when I was boy in Monaghan, they are daily in the farmyard where I live in north County Dublin. Nancy, my late wife, greatly admired John's writing, especially *The Field*. When it was thought an exaggeration that Bull and his wife had not conversed for twenty years, she could name a married couple who addressed each other through a third party, and a second couple who communicated through notes left on the kitchen table. It did not take her half a generation, as it took some critics, to appreciate the work of John B.

In 1966 John submitted the first draft of *The Field* to Phyllis. She read it and handed it on to me, remarking that, 'There's quite a play in there.' How right she was. The script was returned with some suggestions and, in a short time, the finished work was in the post.

Bull McCabe commands the play. The field of the title is for sale. The Bull covets it and when a prospective buyer, William Dee, will not be warned off with words, Bull decides to warn him off with a beating. The beating goes wrong when Tadhg, Bull's son, loses control and Dee is killed. Family loyalty results in a conspiracy of silence and Bull evades the law.

Were Bull no more than a thug who terrorised his locality, we would soon tire of him, but Keane shows us the whole man. Bull is from the frugal years when living was hard. When he protests against four acres of grass being covered by concrete, he speaks for generations who worked the land, and valued it as a trust to be handed on. Nowadays he would wield his ashplant against motorways and super dumps. He would not understand why land that is productive should be covered in tarmacadam for the passage of motor cars, or become a refuse tip for a city that grows no crop and rears no beast to feed a nation.

Bull is a man of imagination – he loves to watch crows – and a man of conscience. When Dee lies dying, he whispers an Act of Contrition in his ear. Or so it was for the opening nights of the first production, but all Ray McAnally's skills could not quell giggles in the audience when he whispered 'Oh my God, I am heartily sorry' into the ear of William Dee. Tension, perhaps, after the brutality of the fight, or disbelief that a man involved in a killing would immediately afterwards kneel to say a prayer in his victim's ear. Whatever the reason, the lines were dropped, something I regretted because they made an important observation about the character of Bull.

For a full understanding of Bull, an audience must wait until the last moments of the play. Alone onstage, shunned by those who lied for his sake, his last thoughts are for William Dee, the murdered man. 'He will be forgot by all,' he says. 'By all except me.' Few last lines are more revealing.

A story I must tell, a confession I must make. Before going into rehearsal I decided that an opening scene was necessary to set up the plot. Looking back, I wonder why I thought of such an aberration, but I did. I got in touch with John, who provided a lively scene at a crossroads. It read well, it acted well, but in no time it was obvious that it added nothing either to the play or to the character of Bull. I had requested the unnecessary. The scene was not used, and I tell the tale because it is included in a manuscript I handed over to the John B. archive in Trinity. No doubt it is a reason for a sideways remark of John's that directors are a strange crowd.

In the first production I played the Bishop. By accident. Richard Hallinan, then business manager of Gemini, Phyllis and myself had completed the casting, or thought we had, when we realised that we had concentrated on the characters directly involved in the action and had forgotten the Bishop. Actors were suggested. Some were not available, others thought unsuitable. Half-joking, Richard said, 'You'd better play it yourself.' A rule of thumb is that a director ought not to act in his own production, but I decided to play the part because it is a solo separated from the main action, and because Ray, who played Bull, agreed to direct me. And because it's a hell of a part.

In his sermon the Bishop appeals for someone to speak so that the murderer of Dee will be identified. If none comes forward, he threatens to put the parish under interdict, a sanction denying the local church the right to celebrate mass or the sacraments under its roof, a penalty of the utmost severity. His threat does not break the conspiracy of silence. Tribal loyalty prevails.

Ray's performance of the Bull was unforgettable. From the threat of his first entrance, when he burst into the pub with the line 'Is ould Maggie Butler in here?' to the searing self-knowledge of the final words, he was a commanding presence. In the years since the first production I have seen excellent performances of the Bull, but (and accepting that because I directed the first production I am open to the charge of prejudice) I have seen none to better Ray.

Groomes Hotel was the place for a drink after the show. Joe Groome and Pattie were warm, welcoming people who vetted their clientele of actors and politicians. Late at night the atmosphere was that of a club. I remember little drunkenness. Rowdiness was not tolerated. Memorable was the occasion when a figure slumped over a table momentarily came to life, hurled a drinks tray across the dining room, then dropped back into somnolence. I was in the company of Donagh MacDonagh, writer and District Justice, the man Brendan Behan joked had a recurring decimal name – DonaghMacDonaghMacDonaghMacDonagh . . . 'Who threw the tray?' I asked. MacDonagh iced his tongue. 'What would you expect from a Fianna Fáil TD from Limerick?'

Civilised behaviour, and a close connection with the ruling party, rendered the hotel immune from after-hours raids, until the midnight hour when a thunder of knocking shocked the gathering into silence. Assuming that some unwelcome client was battering at the door, Pattie opened it a crack, ready to send him packing. To her astonishment, a Sergeant and attendant Guard stepped past her into the lounge. Outraged, Pattie followed – this sort of thing was against the rules.

The Sergeant's notebook appeared. He turned to the first table of drinkers. 'Your name, sir?' Mumble. 'And address?' Mumble. So, too, the second. And the third. Fourth in line was Donagh MacDonagh.

'Your name, sir?'

No mumble this time, but a basilisk glare and a commanding tone, 'I am District Justice Donagh MacDonagh.'

Like a cloud passing over the sun, the Sergeant's expression changed. The calm aspect of magisterial law enforcement gave way to resentment towards the bastard who had delivered him into this booby trap and left him up the creek without a paddle. His notebook closed. His pencil was pocketed. Followed by a sheepish Guard he made for the door. MacDonagh raised his glass. 'The licensing laws in this country are ridiculous,' he said.

Temperance was the habit of my father's house. Intemperance was Saturday night brawls, rowdiness on fair days, rumours of anguish behind drawn blinds and the dissipation of family fortunes. At

Confirmation I took the Pledge, vowing not to drink until I was twenty-one, and broke it when I was a nineteen-year-old university student aping my fellows on Rag Day. For many years I could take a drink or leave it. Mostly I left it. But things changed.

Before rehearsals for *The Field* I visited Ray McAnally to discuss the script. I did not know him very well at the time and his reputation for being difficult went before him. What if he disagreed with me about the play? No director wants a head-to-head with his leading actor, especially when that actor carries far more clout than he does. To brace myself, I stopped for a drink on the way. Or two.

All went well. We were in agreement on every detail of the play and on the character of Bull. I drank a lot of Ray's whiskey without noticing that he was drinking tea, and went home relieved. At the time no one had qualms about drinking and driving.

Ray was a greatly talented actor and a uniquely single-minded man. During a break in rehearsal he told me he had recently joined Alcoholics Anonymous, and had been on the dry for some time. He spoke constantly of AA. He had books on AA. His closest associates were AA members. He played endless AA tapes. Knowing his single-mindedness, I suspected unkindly that, having joined AA, his aim was to be its shining star of sobriety.

When Ray discussed his past drinking I listened intently because, even if I was not prepared to admit it, I had begun to worry about my own. No one sets out to be an alcoholic. No one sets out to get hooked. It was the rapid acceleration of my drinking that sounded alarm bells. From a social drinker I had become a heavy drinker in a surprisingly short time. One drink became two, two became three. After lunch I knocked back a couple, the afternoon break was a dodge to the pub, the end of the working day was time to 'unwind'. Sly drinking crept in when the pace of the rounds was too slow – having a double when the others drank halves, grabbing a quick one on the way to the toilet, lacing a bottle of stout with a whiskey. In time rehearsal commenced with a brandy camouflaged in a cup of coffee, and I did not think it abnormal to drive home swigging from a Baby Power.

I fooled myself that I never showed the signs of drink. I would admit to being 'in good form' but never to being drunk. Drunks fell in the gutter or pestered ladies on the dance floor. Drunks vomited in the street and urinated against shop fronts. Decent people were 'heavy drinkers' – the tippling schoolmaster, the suspended clerk, the wife who embarrassed her husband and got sick in the Ladies, the priest too often in the back room of the local hotel. Such people were 'better class'. The 'alcoholic' was working class, the boozer in the gutter. I was lucky. I did not crash the car. I did not fall on the floor. I did not get into brawls or disgrace myself in public. I did not set fire to the house. I did not estrange my wife.

Knowing one is drinking too much and admitting it are far different. It was not the longer drinking hours afforded by Groomes that speeded me into alcoholism, if I hadn't drunk in Groomes I would have drunk somewhere else. It is the inability to control one's drinking that makes the alcoholic. Compulsion overrides will. It takes life over. But it does not crush pride. Blind drunk, the alcoholic proclaims that he can give it up any time he likes. Pride is the last limpet to cling on.

From Ray I learned that a sure test of control over drink was to go on the dry for a stipulated time, say two weeks. During that time no drink is allowed, no matter what the circumstance. It is succeed or fail.

I put myself on the dry for two weeks. The first day was an adventure. The second tolerable. By the third I was struggling. It was a Saturday, during the run of *The Field*. The Bishop does not appear until the second act, and I had no need to change into costume until the first interval. Normally, for such had normality become, I had a quick one before going backstage, and a Baby Power in my pocket to keep me going during the show. On the third evening I went straight to my dressing room but was too uneasy to remain there. When the house lights dimmed, I went out front and stood at the back of the auditorium. But I could not concentrate on the play. Or on anything but the door at my side that opened into the bar. I felt weak. I leaned against the wall. Sweat poured down my face. When I could bear it no longer I slipped into the bar.

I got through the performance, but the rest of the night is a haze. I remember going to Ray and appealing for help, and of going to Groomes to drink until Donal, Ray's AA contact, arrived. I have no idea what we discussed, but before we parted he gave me the time of an AA meeting in Ranelagh next morning. Later he told me that he did not expect me to turn-up, but I did, feeling wretched, embarrassed and demeaned. Donal introduced me to those present. I was given a cup of tea. No one asked questions. No one pushed me.

When the meeting began I heard for the first time the words with which the chairman commences a meeting, words with which I would soon be familiar, 'My name is X. I am an alcoholic.' I am not sure how much I took in at that first meeting – I was far too distressed to listen attentively – but gradually I realised that I was amongst those who had been through what I was going through, that they understood, and that help was at hand if I was willing to accept it.

Those who have no problem with drink have no understanding of the alcoholic. Heavy drinkers, bouters (those who break-out every now and then for a couple of weeks) and let-the-hair-down night-outers are a different breed. Only alcoholics fully understand the compulsion of alcoholism. They are not outside observers, they are experts who have learned the hard way. I believe that from the night I called on Ray to discuss *The Field*, he suspected that I had a problem, and was waiting in the hope of being on hand when the distress call sounded. It was my good fortune that he was.

After that first AA meeting I never drank again. This was no miracle conversion. He who is converted has within him a longing, an inclination, towards a particular desire. My desire was sobriety. What I required was impetus and I got it from AA. To that organisation and to Ray I am forever humbly indebted.

I settled with relief into the AA routine. It was not always easy. I had to learn what it was to live a day at a time. For an alcoholic to promise to give up drink for life is beyond imagining – day after day, month after month, year after year, who could face that prospect? But not to drink for a day is conceivable. Or an hour. Or a minute. Or, as was once my desperate resort, a mile at a time. I was driving to a meeting. The pubs were open. I needed a drink. All I had to do was stop. To think a day at a time was too much, I wouldn't last half a day. So I concentrated on the speedometer, promising that after the next mile I would stop at the nearest pub. And when that mile was reached, I tried again. And again. A mile at a time. And so, mile by mile, I reached the meeting and refuge from the pursuing demons.

An unexpected hurdle remained, one I had not anticipated. There is no formal chairman of an AA group. The day came when I was asked to take the chair. The opening words do not vary, 'My name is X. I am an alcoholic.' Listening to others it seemed easy. Now it was my turn. I accepted that I was an alcoholic, but in my mind, privately. Now I must speak the word out loud. To a gathering of sober men and women I must say, 'My name is Barry. I am an alcoholic.'

No words I have ever spoken in public were so difficult to utter. I had to force them out. But when they were spoken I felt, astonishingly, that I had moved to a new plane of honesty. Lingering evasions were routed. The word 'alcoholic' spoken aloud was not an admission of shame, it was a protective shield. No longer had I any doubt about where I stood.

Friends, with all the sympathy, or the embarrassment, of the uninformed, assure me that I was never an alcoholic. I don't argue. It doesn't matter. It is enough that, since 1966, I have not had a drink, and that I and those around me are the better for it. A day at a time. So far so good.

I secured a place for my father in Beaumont Nursing Home in Dublin. After elaborate thanks to the Matron, and a backhand apology by way of a joke about causing her a lot of trouble, he was carried on a stretcher to the ambulance that would drive him to Dublin.

Before leaving, I said my thanks to the Matron. In a duty-for-the-love-of-God voice she answered, 'We did our best.'

I too was chilly. 'I understand.'

Did I chide her because she was an undemonstrative woman wearing an unworldly habit? Or because I must defend my father? Since he had given me his attaché case of souvenirs, our roles had altered: he had put himself in my care; his late years were mine to make smooth.

As usual, new surroundings raised his spirits, but this time he did not live long enough for the gilt to wear off. When he was shaving he slipped and fell. Twenty-four hours later, and not until then, it was discovered that he had broken his hip. He was moved to Jervis Street Hospital and prepared for an operation. The surgeon did not minimise the risk, 'His heart is strong but at eighty-six it is not the broken hip that is the danger but the shock of the operation.'

A date for the operation was set, then postponed. 'A bit of a cold,' my father told me. 'The chest. Something to do with the anaesthetic.' Anxiously he added, 'The sooner it's over, the better.' For the first time I began to think that he might die. If he did, I must be with him at the end. I owed him that.

The operation was again planned, and again postponed. Twice I was called to Jervis Street in expectation of his death. Each time he rallied, but his death would come soon, and before the end I had a duty to perform. That I considered it a duty saddened me, but that is too often the way with sons and fathers, expressions of affection stick in the throat, and years of unease drag on until age intervenes and an old man is dying. I was my father's only son, his white-haired boy. He had supported me when I joined the theatre, had admired what success I had, but looking out a window and furtive glances at my watch had become a habit of communication.

Throughout the weeks of his illness I was rehearsing for the first production of John B.'s *Big Maggie*, scheduled to open in the Cork Opera House, and return to the Olympia. On the day I was to leave for Cork I sat by his bed. I knew what I must say, had thought it out from the moment I feared he might not survive. Each day I had gone to his bedside intending to speak, wanting to, but always postponing the moment, hoping even as I left the hospital, that I had not delayed too long and that he would not die before my next visit.

The moment that separates tight lips from an open heart is a test of resolution too often failed. We vacillate and look to the future, but my father had no future and ahead of me was only guilt if I did not speak. I looked into the eyes I had so long avoided, and gathered myself to release the words so long imprisoned. 'I am grateful for all you did for me,' I said. 'I love you.'

He took my hand. We knew we were saying goodbye.

I drove south, carrying Phyllis Ryan and Marie Kean as passengers. The journey was slow. I had brought my usual luggage, so too had Phyllis, but Marie included the kitchen sink, the kitchen itself, the family silver and the sideboard. The car lay low like an overloaded tramp steamer labouring through a heavy swell, the exhaust whacking the ground when I crossed a humpback bridge.

I worried all the way. What if my father died over the weekend? What then of the show? Even to have harboured such a thought seems heartless, but the ruthless discipline of the theatre was ingrained in me – death, tempest or calamity, the curtain must go up on time. Such thinking is a distortion of responsibility, a self-drama-tising confusion of priorities. Had my father died I would, of course, have come home. The lighting of the show would have been taken over by the designer Patrick Murray and the dress rehearsal supervised by Phyllis and Mai McFall, that most excellent of stage directors. *Maggie* would gave gone onstage as ably as if I were present.

The night before *Maggie* opened, *The Late Late Show* featured a scene from the play, that in which Maggie (Marie Kean) berates Katie (Liz Davis) for having spent time in a bedroom of the local hotel with the ill-reputed Toss Melch. (Toss Melch – what a name, sleaze and seduction oozing from every syllable.)

John B.'s name and exposure on the *Late Late* had an immediate effect. On Monday morning rain streamed down but when the box office opened a queue had already formed, a queue that did not break until the house had sold out for the week.

The first night swept along on a high tide of excitement. From the moment the play settled, there was never a doubt that Gemini and John B. were on to a winner. The trickiest scene in the play is that between Maggie and Teddy Heelin, the commercial traveller. Teddy is a womaniser, the sort of man who thinks every woman is Mount Everest and must be climbed. Too often the mistake is made of putting size first when casting Maggie, overlooking that it is in personality that Maggie is big, not necessarily in size. If Maggie is not played by an attractive woman the scene between herself and Teddy becomes grotesque, and the play is distorted. It is a tricky scene, and we were still experimenting with it at one o'clock on the Saturday we were due to leave for Cork. Marie brought things to a halt. 'No time for any more,' she said. 'We must stick with what we have. The first night will tell us a lot.' It did. The moment the audience realised that Teddy had turned his attentions to Maggie, the house rocked, and the players had to fight for control. The laughter was not the laughter of derision so much as the laughter of astonishment. Afterwards Gerry Sullivan, who played Teddy, summed it up by saying, 'It was like riding a bucking bronco out there.'

Maggie broke the house record in Cork, came to Dublin and did it again in the Olympia. The run was scheduled to finish after seven weeks when Marie was contracted to make a film, but the success was so great that the run was extended, with Joan O'Hara taking over. Unruffled, the box office jingled merrily on. After a break *Maggie* went on tour with Doreen Hepburn playing Maggie. Next came Anna Manahan, who played the part for months to ever-full houses.

There are star actors who draw the crowds and there are star plays. *Big Maggie* is a star. She caught the public imagination. She is larger than life, a woman whose acerbic tongue makes an audience gasp and sit forward in their seats. She is a tigress who protects her young against all comers, and, when the time is ripe, drives them from her to fend for themselves. Tough love. Women relish Maggie. Men dodge when they see her in the street.

Between runs and revivals, *Maggie* ran for over a year, until it seemed that, for the moment at least, it was exhausted. But there was life in the lady still. I was rehearsing for a Gemini season in Limerick when Phyllis announced that the Olympia wanted *Maggie* again. But how? Most of the cast were engaged for Limerick and rehearsal dates overlapped. *Maggie* was demanded and must take the stage. And so she did, with Ronnie Masterson as Maggie, a new cast and myself shuttling between rehearsal rooms, preparing for the season in Limerick and for the performance in the Olympia.

On opening night I took my usual place at the back of the auditorium, wondering if *Maggie* had been revived once too often. I need not have worried. The first comedy line raised its usual laugh, the first scene-drop won its usual enthusiastic hand. Phyllis was beside me. 'It's off again,' she said. And so it was. *Maggie* was irrepressible.

Three weeks after I returned to Dublin from Cork, my father died. Several times he was on the brink of death but had recovered. Until the end he was lucid. A few days before his death he summoned the ward sister, a nun. 'Am I dying?' he asked. 'Yes,' she answered.

Her answer contented him. With death approaching, he prayed a lot. At times he lapsed into sleep or unconsciousness and it seemed that his time was at hand. But always he revived, to turn his eyes on those at his bedside and to live on.

I was not present when a patient across the ward said, 'I think that man is dead.' My father's eyes opened. 'I'm damn well not,' he said. 'Not yet.'

My sisters gathered, Maureen from Balbriggan, Toni from Cork and Vera from England. Hour after hour I sat by his bed or smoked in the corridor outside the ward. Days passed. Time after time his great strength pulled him back from the brink. Eventually Toni's and Vera's leaves of absence were exhausted and they had to return to work, leaving the vigil to Maureen and myself.

Fatigue numbs the mind and the emotions. I do not recall feelings of grief. What I recall is the fatigue of keeping vigil. 'Go for a meal,' a sister advised. Maureen and I were doubtful. 'He has rallied again,' she said. 'There is no immediate danger.'

We decided to drive to Salmon for a meal and then return. I was opening the hall door when I heard the phone and needed no one to tell me what had happened. Christ, after all the waiting, he died when my back was turned.

Screens were around his bed when we returned. 'He sat up and looked around,' we were told. 'Then he fell back.' Was he looking for me? I had nothing left to offer him but my presence at his death and that had been denied. Never had I felt so vilely cheated.

When he was laid out, I sat by his bed, recalling the long years when I found it impossible to reciprocate the joy he found in me. Too late I was contrite. In time the tears would come. Why do we cry for the dead? Tears will not bring them back. We cry for ourselves, for our loss, for pettiness and wrongs done that cannot be righted. And we cry for happy moments in the past that we will frame and cherish to lighten the burden of guilty remembrance.

Before he died my father made a last request. Written in his notepad was a résumé of his career in the Post Office, followed by the years he served in France in the Great War. 'Get it into the paper for me,' he requested. Through a friend in the newspaper business I did, in a prominent position in a national newspaper. At least I could do that for him.

I think the Great War always remained close to the surface of his thoughts. It may have been the zenith of his life, the point of keenest living. Before he died, he bequeathed to me his copy of A. J. P. Taylor's *The First World War*. In the margins he had made notes, one of which read, 'I remember the second day of this attack. It was my birthday.' And on another page, 'I was on The Somme on the 20th but I didn't stay very long. With the rest I ran like hell.'

The most telling entry was on the flyleaf. In writing grown unsteady with age he had inscribed, '165695 John Cassin, Royal Engineers, Signals, attached Cavalry and Tank Corps, France 1916 – 1919'. Studying the entry it was not difficult to understand why, at the age of thirty-four, when he was climbing the civil service ladder and with a family to support, my father volunteered to fight in France. His reason was uncomplicated. The British civil service had given him his livelihood. King and country was his creed, defending it his duty.

I carried my father's coffin and walked behind the hearse. To those beside me I made nervy jokes and was not calm until the grave was filled in. A meal was arranged for family and friends but I did not attend. I stayed at home with Nancy. 'I don't want to talk to people,' I said. In her quiet way she answered, 'I understand.'

Later I laid my hand on the attaché case that held his souvenirs. But I did not open it. All that was over.

6

For so long known as an actress, it came as a surprise when the grapevine rumoured that Phyllis Ryan was preparing to manage a show in the Gas Company Theatre, Dun Laoghaire. But on the show went, in 1956, under the name of Orion Productions. A couple of years later, she and Norman Rodway joined forces and the company was renamed Gemini, which title was retained when Norman moved permanently to London with the Gemini success of *Stephen D*, Hugh Leonard's adaptation from Joyce.

Gradually Phyllis's influence extended and from the late fifties until the eighties Gemini was a major force in the Irish theatre. In my long association with the company I directed fifty, sixty, God knows how many plays in the Gate, the Olympia, the Gaiety, the Cork Opera House, on tour and in America. The company base was the

Eblana, a small theatre in the basement of Busáras, designed as a news-reel cinema to entertain travellers awaiting departure. To my knowledge it never opened as a cinema and lay empty but for occasional use by adventurous fringe groups, including a forgettable revue presented by Nora Lever and myself, its only claim to fame that it gave a job to a beginner called Rosaleen MacMenamin, who would become a star under her married name of Rosaleen Linehan.

The theatre lay dungeon-dark and unexplored for many years until it was taken over by Phyllis Ryan. That she succeeded in making it an important part of Dublin theatre life is a tribute to her tenacity and keen theatrical instinct. Under her management the Eblana staged the work of playwrights ranging from Tennessee Williams to Neil Simon, from Alan Ayckbourn to Edward Albee, and included the play with the lengthiest title I know, *Oh Dad, Poor Dad, Mamma's Hung You in the Closet and I'm Feelin' So Sad*.

Many Irish authors found a stage in the Eblana, including Eugene McCabe, Tom Coffey, David Hayes, Harry Barton and Patrick Galvin. In 1966, as part of the 1916 commemorations, McCabe's play *Pull Down a Horseman* was presented. A lengthy one-act, splendidly acted by Niall Toibin and T. P. McKenna, it was an imaginary conversation between Padraig Pearse and James Connolly, supposedly at the time of the Rising. The second part of the bill, a memory of the Great War, was assembled by Eamon Keane. A tableau from the production was that of a line of Tommies, some on one knee firing rifles, some casting hand-grenades, others advancing across No Man's Land, images I set up from memories of my father's book of photographs of trench life. Among the line of young actors who played the Tommies were Alan Devlin, Frank Grimes and Joe Dowling, a future artistic Director of the Abbey before moving to

Minneapolis to run that distinguished playhouse.

A feature of Gemini's Eblana years were the immensely successful Fergus Linehan revues which ran forever. Regulars in the casts were Rosaleen Linehan, Des Keogh, David Kelly, Anna Manahan, Frank Kelly, Bill Golding and Jim Norton, no mean comedy team to greet on the first morning of rehearsal.

Working with Gemini I was always assured of a quality cast; Norman Rodway, Jim Norton, Maureen Toal, David Kelly, Arthur O'Sullivan, Joe Lynch, Ray McAnally, Ronnie Masterson, Rosaleen Linehan, Marie Kean, T. P. McKenna, Niall Toibin, Anna Manahan, Eamon Morrissey, Maria McDermottroe, Barbara Brennan, Robert Carrickford, and Martin Dempsey, to name but a few, and, before *Yes, Minister* was even a glint in its author's eye, Nigel Hawthorne, who played in the Gate in *Come Blow Your Horn*.

In the Olympia I directed the first Irish productions of Arthur Miller's *The Price* and Edward Albee's *Who's Afraid of Virginia Woolf?*, with T. P. McKenna and Katherine Blake, a triple award-winner in Canada. With particular pleasure I recall Hugh Leonard's adaptation of Joyce's 'The Dead'. It was staged for the Dublin Theatre Festival as the second half of a double bill, *The Quick and the Dead*, the first half a contemporary comedy by Leonard entitled *The Late Arrival of the Incoming Aircraft*. The set of *The Dead* was designed by Patrick Murray, and the actors, led by Jim Norton and Maureen Toal, caught every nuance of that flawless story.

The opening was delicate; in the background the notes of a muted piano, while light fell angularly on the exterior of a Georgian window, through it drifting 'the snow that was falling all over Ireland.' When the curtain went up, there was a spontaneous round of applause. Beside me was Patrick Murray, a man of irrepressible good humour.

Into my ear he hissed, 'They'll take that back when they see the rest of the set.'

A device I introduced into the performance became known in the jargon of rehearsal as 'the freeze'. To indicate a passage of time, on a given cue the actors froze in position, the lighting changed, and in the background the piano gently played. The effect was of a fading sepia photograph that stirs the past with wistful nostalgia. I'm sure I was not the first to use such a device and I won't be the last; art is carried on the shoulders of those who have gone before.

There is a coda to my story of *The Dead*. The reaction of the critics was not what I had hoped, and I was nursing my disappointment when I received a letter from Michael Mac Liammóir, full of admiration for the performance. A few nights later I met him backstage in one of the theatres and immediately thanked him, adding how encouraging I found his words, in view of the indifference of the critics. A benevolent hand was rested on my shoulder and I awaited the Master's words. In Michael's most mellifluous tones they came, 'My dear Barry, the critics? Fuck them.'

The previous year, in the Gaiety, I had directed *Dublin One*, adaptations from the *Dubliners* stories given unity by Hugh Leonard's skill in weaving them around the character of Mr Kiernan. I regret that since then no management has paid tribute to Joyce, and to his most sensitive adapter, Hugh Leonard, by presenting a choice from *Dublin One* as the first half of a bill and concluding the evening with *The Dead*.

Phyllis Ryan could have looked to other theatres for an engagement as artistic director but she chose to run her own show. She undertook the artistic direction of the Irish Theatre Company when it was formed, but only for six months before returning to Gemini.

For many years her skills enticed leading authors to submit new scripts to Gemini rather than to the National Theatre; a compliment to Phyllis and a reflection on the Abbey of the time, which did not attract new writing as a national theatre should. But with the building of the new theatre and the appointments of Tomás Mac Anna to the main theatre and Joe Dowling to the Peacock, artistic directorship was forward-thinking; new writers were encouraged and the National Theatre was again, as it ought always to have been, the leader in the development of new Irish writing. Authors who had previously turned to independent companies now looked to the Abbey, with the result that gradually the artistic fortunes of Gemini declined.

Memories are short. Too few are now aware of Phyllis Ryan's success, or the range of theatre brought to Dublin by Gemini Productions, a remarkable achievement in a business littered with the bankrupt corpses of independent managements.

In a long association with Phyllis I never knew her to complain when business was bad. On an occasion in Limerick when the first two weeks of a summer season played to poor business, and backstage gossip feared the worst, I asked her for how long the company could survive. 'Until the end of the season,' she snapped. I should have known better than to ask.

The first John B. Keane play I directed for Gemini was *The Highest House on the Mountain*, the last *The Chastitute*. In the twenty years between came *No More in Dust*, *The Field*, *Big Maggie*, *The Change in Mame Fadden* and *The Good Thing*, all first productions. Neither *Mame Fadden* nor *The Good Thing* was a big success, and neither, to my knowledge, has been professionally revived. For Noel Pearson I directed *Many Young Men of Twenty* with Joe Lynch, and in Tralee, with the local amateur players I directed *The Crazy Wall*, an autobiographical piece that deserved attention from the professional theatre.

Keane was a laugh-maker among the best. In *The Chastitute* he is at his most light-hearted, upending pathos to create comedy. A chastitute, he declares, is the opposite of a prostitute. The play recounts the woes and tribulations of a repressed man, desperate to lose his virginity. But there is more to the play than fall-on-your-arse farce. John Bosco is not a gormless clown, nor is he a sex maniac. He is one of a generation of John Boscos who craved a woman's love and companionship but knew not how to find it; sad figures, Paddy Maguires who grew old spilling their longings into the fading embers of the dying turf, victims of ignorance, fear and repression. Playing the part of John Bosco, Donal Farmer lurched with sensitivity and a fine sense of comedy from one misfortune to the next, emphasising the pathos and allowing the comedy to look after itself.

Keane's ability to switch effortlessly from the serious to the comic was not always to the taste of his critics. Fashion had it that the author of *The Field* lowered his standards with *Moll* and *The Chastitute*, as if his versatility was an imperfection. I might add that around the time he was taking the world by storm, I attended a series of lectures on the theatre delivered in one of our universities, and there listened to a lecturer explain that how *not* to write a play was how John B. Keane wrote one. Academic opinion did not worry the public; put the name of John B. on a billboard and they flocked in. Critics and the public inhabit different worlds. Plays that received excellent notices have emptied the house, plays that were slammed have played tunes of glory at the box office.

When a production fails, a scapegoat must be found. The

playwright blames the director, the director blames the play, the actors blame everyone from the publicity man to the conjunction of Mars and Venus on the night the cow jumped over the moon. Everyone blames the bloody critics. When a critic gives a favourable notice, he is sensitive and informed, when he gives a bad one he is an illiterate football reporter. (Football reporters please forgive.) The critic assesses the artistic merit of a play, the public look for entertainment. No one rushes to book seats when the voice on the mobile says, 'I was at t'Abbey last night. Oh *Jaysus!*'

Criticism in the theatre, as in all artistic fields, is necessary, even salutary, but if notices are mixed, where does one stand? If I disagree with a review that is critical, am I entitled to walk tall when I read one that is favourable? Coliseum bloodbaths such as, *Katharine Hepburn ran through the gamut of emotions from A to B* or *Last night Tallulah Bankhead as Cleopatra barged down the Nile and promptly sank* make entertaining bitchery, but to be on the receiving end is no joke. On a memorable occasion I got the ultimate slam when a critic wrote that 'the play succeeded in spite of the direction'. That drew blood. So I left reading notices to those with thicker skins. It wasn't easy. Like giving up fags, there was the temptation to have a sly drag in the jax when I heard that the notices were good, but I persevered until no critical nicotine stained my sensitive soul.

Acceptance by the Abbey brought with it a welcome critical reversal when John B.'s early dismissal as a folksy rural commentator was replaced by recognition of his rightful place in the canon of Irish writing. Before breaching the citadel of the National Theatre, he had a long and painful wait. In 1962, the Abbey staged *Hut 42*, not the most successful of his plays. Prior to acceptance by the Abbey, it had been offered to other managements. Illsley-McCabe asked me to read the script, but I turned it down. The play needed a lot of reworking, and whatever hope of success it would have had with Gemini, who had a sure touch for Keane, I doubted if it would succeed in the hands of Illsley-McCabe.

Phyllis Ryan and Gemini Productions made a major contribution to the success of John B. Keane. It can be argued that if Phyllis had not accepted his plays, someone else would have. In fact, while *The Field* and *Big Maggie* were filling the Olympia and the Cork Opera House for Gemini, James N. Healy and his Southern Theatre Company of Cork were travelling to Dublin with *Sharon's Grave*, *The Man from Clare* and *Moll*. While readily admitting to personal prejudice because of my long association with Phyllis, I believe that the production levels of Gemini were greater than those of the Southern Theatre Company. That aside, however worthily Keane was served by both companies, the place for a playwright of national importance is within the walls of his national theatre, and Keane had a long wait before delayed justice was done when the Abbey staged *Sive*, in 1984 and went on to revive a number of his plays. The publican from Listowel had outstayed his detractors.

Across my heart, branded in letters of blood, is the title *Cemented with Love*. Written by Sam Thompson, the author of *Over the Bridge*, which had caused a storm in Belfast, the script came to Gemini about a year after *The Field*. The problem with the production was not technical. It was human. The leading actor was Ray McAnally, an actor with a reputation for making life difficult for directors. When things went his way, as they did during *The Field*, the sun shone merrily, when they did not, thunderclouds hung low over the rehearsal room.

In this production things did not go his way.

Sam Thompson was an author who came straight to the point; if the script was rough at the edges, there was no mistaking the message. That was good enough for me, but not for Ray. From the moment rehearsal began, he suggested changes, not merely a line here or there but whole scenes to be rewritten. Where the re-writes were to come from I had no idea, because Sam Thompson had died some years previously. Undeterred, Ray undertook to do the re-writes himself, and I was transported to his home to approve of his alterations. Whether I approved or not did not enter into it, because at the first hint of change neither Phyllis Ryan nor Mrs Thompson, Sam's widow, was prepared to allow anyone a free rein with the text. Arguments followed. Management did not wilt. Ray's mood darkened. Storm clouds gathered. Brendan Smith, the Festival Director, visited the rehearsal room. There were whisperings in corners. The phone line hummed between Dublin and Belfast. Mrs Thompson's agent entered the fray, and it was rumoured that the play would be withdrawn.

Refused his re-writes, Ray zoned in on the character he was playing. In the script there was mention that the man had had a heart attack – a hint, no more. I had not given the matter much thought; heart attack or no heart attack, the plot was not affected, and I was happy to push along untroubled by the character's cardiac condition. Not Ray. He demanded an answer. Did the man have a heart attack or did he not? Ignore him, I thought, get on with the play and ignore him. Some hope. Ray was not a man to be ignored. The rehearsal room twanged with tension, and I found myself the focus of Ray's frustration. Every discussion, every tea break was dominated by heart attack or no heart attack. Attempting to dismiss the matter was impossible – heart attack or no heart attack became a cause, a battle to be won, and I was in the line of fire.

'Don't let him get to you,' Phyllis advised. Too late. He had already got to me. Every morning on the way to rehearsal, I prayed that the play would be cancelled, or that Ray would withdraw, or that the theatre would burn down – anything to remove this cross from me. I could have handed back the script, cried off, invented a personal heart attack, walked out. But I don't walk out. I stick with things to the bitter end. Why? God knows. Training? Martyrdom? False loyalty? Maybe all three. I could even have had a showdown. Which, unexpected and unplanned, is eventually what happened.

Ray, Ronnie Masterson, myself and one other were in the rehearsal room. The rest of the cast had gone to lunch. Or taken cover. Cups of tea were distributed and yet again Ray zoned in on heart attack or no heart attack. I protested that there was no evidence in the script one way or the other and that Ray must decide for himself. What I left unsaid, but which must have been obvious in every exasperated syllable I uttered, was that it was time he bloody well shut up about it and got on with the shaggin' play.

An Atlantic storm rolled in. Did I not understand the problems of the actor? How was he expected to give a rounded characterisation with such a vital piece of evidence missing? And on and on and on . . .

I have always been afflicted by a quick, explosive temper. I hold things in, say nothing, grind, then in an unguarded instant I am shouting. In my hand was a tea cup. Without warning I hurled it to the floor.

Stunned silence.

Then farce. The rehearsal room was large and bare. The floor was convent-shiny. The cup was made of plastic. It did not break. It rattled across the floor, hit the wall and rattled back again. It seemed to rattle on forever. When it came to rest, it lay on the polished floor, as incongruous as a carbuncle on the unblemished hide of a *Playboy* centrefold.

Everyone stared at the cup. Then the merciful God of good sense came to our rescue. We laughed. Nervous, shaky laughter, but laughter all the same.

No more was heard of heart attacks. The sun returned from its winter occlusion and the rehearsal room basked in a heat wave of good fellowship. The play opened to good notices and – need I say it? – Ray gave a splendid performance.

A happier experience of working with Ray – one of many, let me emphasise – was the first production of John B. Keane's *The Matchmaker*, which, in a convoluted way, reminds me of the visit to Dublin of John F. Kennedy. It was brought into focus when I met Milo O'Shea, who was in Dublin making a film. He recalled that with a group of actors we were waiting at the Gate to see JFK pass. The city – the country – was ablaze with excitement. Those too young to remember the Kennedy years do not understand the astonishing impact he made. He was a shining light in the grim Cold War years, he defied the Soviet Union across the Berlin Wall, he stood firm during the Cuban Missile Crisis, he was hope in a bleak world.

Milo and I grabbed a spot on the porch over the entrance to the theatre to catch a view of this bronzed god from all-powerful America. When the cavalcade arrived, Kennedy was on his feet, smiling and waving. Reaching the theatre he looked up and, Milo claimed, had a special wave for the welcoming thespians.

Preceding and following Kennedy were transports laden with security men who scanned footpaths, windows, roofs and parapets, the bulge of firearms nestling in ready holsters. We smiled. This was Dublin, for God's sake, who would threaten Kennedy in Dublin? Wasn't he one of our own? On that night of heady celebration none could foresee that, from a top window in Dallas, Lee Harvey Oswald would write his name into history alongside that of John Wilkes Booth.

No doubt in time Kennedy's golden promise would have tarnished, but he was cut down before the dream faded. Nowadays cynicism deals only with his womanising and the sensation of his death, but those of us who lived during his truncated presidency remember the hope he generated and the torrent of grief that followed his assassination. Out of this sprang the play *Kennedy's Children*, by Robert Patrick, a lament for the loss of direction felt by many Americans following his death. In 1975 Ray booked the Eblana for a season and chose to open with *Kennedy's Children*, only to learn that the tidal wave of emotion generated by Kennedy's death had subsided and the public had moved on. I attended the first night, and as early as the interval two theatre managers, wise in the ways of the public, shook their heads.

A few days later I heard from Ray. Things were going badly. How badly? Very badly. What was he to do? Run for your life, I advised. Running for your life is all very well if you have somewhere to run to, but Ray's confidence in *Kennedy's Children* was such that he had booked the Eblana for fourteen weeks without a back-up production to replace it if it failed. His problem was more than the failure of a play, he had bet house and home on *Kennedy's Children* and the horse had fallen at the first fence. The play could be taken off in a week but what was to follow?

Ronnie and himself must rescue the situation. If they got something together, would I direct? Of course – anything to bail out the sinking ship. What had he in mind? He and Ronnie would do excerpts from plays, character studies, a ballad or two, a bit of this, a bit of that. Old scripts would be dug out. Comic recitations would be trawled from the depths of memory. Scenes from O'Casey would be given a whirl, and Ray might even brush up his skills with the guitar, studied for *The Golden Years*, and include a Percy French selection.

Disasterville, I thought. Without sufficient time to research and construct a show properly I doubted if even Ray's reputation would attract an audience for a night of bits and pieces. But needs must, hope springs eternal and all that jazz, and – miracle of miracles – perhaps something could be cobbled together that would temporarily stave off the bank manager until a play could be rehearsed to replace *Kennedy's Children*.

By Friday the prospect was grim. We were still discussing ideas when Phyllis Ryan arrived without warning, a slim volume in her hand. 'Have a look at this,' she said, and was gone again.

The slim volume was *Letters of a Matchmaker*, the latest addition to John B. Keane's *Letters* series. Ray read some pages and handed it to me. 'We might get twenty minutes out of it.' We read on – 'We might get half a show out of it.' We read to the end. The penny dropped. Between the covers was a full show and, more than that, a new show by John B. Keane. (In retrospect, I suspect that Phyllis read *Letters of a Matchmaker* with a thought of doing it herself, but knowing Ray's predicament generously passed on the idea.)

John B. was contacted for permission to adapt and, considerate as ever to friends in need, said carry on. Then it was mugs of coffee and Ronnie's typewriter clattering. Between Friday evening and the following Monday *Matchmaker* was edited into a one-and-a-half hour show. There was no hope of Ray or Ronnie memorising the lines in time for the opening, so it was arranged that they would sit at tables and the performance would be presented as 'A Reading'.

Bob Heade came up with a set hung with spider's webs – the Matchmaker's address is 'Spiders Well' – and on Monday night, little more than three days after Phyllis had handed the script to Ray, *Matchmaker* opened with fingers crossed and a best hope that it would provide breathing space for a couple of weeks until a new play could be found and rehearsed.

Part of the fun of *Matchmaker* was that it was played by two actors required to switch character from letter to letter as adroitly as a quick-change artist changes costume. Ray revelled in it, pulling out all the stops in a joyous display of versatility. The woman's part (or parts) is less showy, but Ronnie's playing was the perfect foil to Ray's flamboy-ance. In a week or so the lines were memorised, but throughout the run the format of 'A Reading' was maintained.

Within a couple of nights the house was full, and the play ran for twelve weeks, hardly dropping a seat. *Letters of a Matchmaker* had suc-ceeded beyond the wildest of our wildest dreams. The McAnally hearth and home was rescued from the bailiff. John B. had done it again.

Ray was a man of ideas. His restless mind was never off duty. When he interested himself in a subject, it was not enough to understand it, he must master it. As much concentration went into golf as into the study of a script, or into a theological discourse (he was very good at that sort of thing) or the planning of Ronnie's kitchen when they moved house.

Twice when he was working in England I received distress calls late at night. The first when he was playing in London in *The Mighty Reservoy*, a two-man play by Peter Terson, the second when he was engaged by John Clements for a summer season in Chichester. He did not have to explain why he'd called. A phone call from an AA colleague under pressure demands a response. It is networking, a lifeline against the temptation of the bottle. Ray's call from London was that the director was an idiot incapable of handling the script. In Chichester nothing escaped his vitriol – the theatre, the productions, the acting, the colour of the walls. Right or wrong was not the point; his phone calls were a cry for help and I had an opportunity to repay him for introducing me to AA.

At times of depression and hyper-tension it seemed that something must give – a heart attack or a mental breakdown. But he appeared to draw energy from these bouts. None escaped his posturing, and much of the time I believe he was posturing. Performers seek attention, and Ray was a performer not only on stage but in public, by turns master-actor, charmer and adviser with part of him, like an actor onstage, standing aside to modulate his performance. I doubt if he would have admitted to such a charge, equally I doubt if a man of such analytical powers could totally deceive himself. It may be that I totally misread his moods. If I do, it is in an effort to understand, not to condemn.

He longed for fame – or more correctly, I believe, for recognition of his talent. Ireland viewed him as an outstanding actor, but he sought a wider field where his gift would receive the appreciation it deserved. International recognition came late with the film *The Mission* and on television with *A Very British Coup*. His time ought to have come earlier when he played *Who's Afraid of Virginia Woolf?* in

London, but drink seriously impeded his progress. That he overcame alcoholism and re-established what could have been a lost career must be credited to his unwavering determination and self-belief. A heart attack did not slow him down. At last the big, lucrative engagements were rolling in and he worked nonstop. Foreseeing a terminal attack, I am told he remarked that Sutton, his local church, would not be big enough for the funeral and that the Pro-Cathedral would be required. He was right. It was packed to overflowing.

His death deeply grieved me. At his best he was entertaining, helpful, and invigorating company. Memories of good days and bad in his company shuffle like a deck of cards when I remember fourballs with Edmund Brown and Vernon Hayden, directing him and being directed by him, arguing about every subject from morality to the tennis champion Jimmy Connors. I do not airbrush the tense rehearsal rooms, his aggressive ego, or the pain I sadly witnessed him cause others. And could not excuse. And told him so. But genuine friendship must endure through more than easy times and sunny days.

His funeral in the Pro-Cathedral was huge. He lay in his coffin in full make-up. Centre-stage to the end.

7

I made my return to acting in the Lyric Theatre, Belfast in 1995. I had travelled North to meet David Grant to discuss a part in *The Crucible*, only to be told when I arrived that the part was already cast. So why had I been allowed to come all the way from Dublin? Because David's fellow director, Robin Midgley, was looking for an actor for a new play and would like to talk to me. The play was *Lengthening Shadows*, the role that of a ninety-nine-year-old retired RUC officer. The author was Graham Reid, a razor-sharp observer of the Northern scene. A Belfast accent was required, but I had done my schooling in Monaghan and worked enough in the Lyric to have no fears on that score. It was a glance through the script that worried me. The part was a mile long, and after so many years of directing I feared that I may have lost the trick of memorising lines. Gone were the days when I knocked off lines in the bus or at halftime at a football match; in their place were hours of agonising over a single word – was it 'insignificant', 'inconsiderable' or 'inconsequential'? Yellow sticky notes were pasted to the bathroom mirror, to the car windscreen, to the television screen. I chanted the word like a cultish mantra until it was securely memorised. Then it evaporated and I must start again.

It would have been easy to find an excuse and refuse the part, but if I did, if I funked it, the time had come to shut the make-up box and retire into the anecdotal years. But not yet, I decided. Memorising the lines might be blood, sweat and tears, but the part was magnificent and hell or high water I intended to play it.

Lengthening Shadows ran for three and a half weeks, the normal Lyric run, and I had some success in the part, which led to a number of engagements in theatre, the most interesting being David Grant's updated *The Merchant of Venice*, in which I played the Prince as a Mafia Godfather returning from a meeting of the Dons, attired in evening dress, wearing an overcoat with an astrakhan collar, top hat, silk scarf, and sporting a silver-headed cane. Apart from playing the Prince, I played Tubal and Old Gobbo and spent more time changing costume than I did on stage. Doubling-up, it's called. Fun, if one enjoys whipping off one costume to don the next, using a moustache for this character, a beard for that, and altering the voice (hopefully) in an effort to disguise that it is the same actor under a different guise – some hope for anyone of my height.

David encouraged actors to do warm-ups before rehearsal; walk rapidly, turn sharply, reverse, etc. I was never an enthusiast for warm-ups, but I earned Brownie points for trying. Limbering-up I leave to the young and fit. Neither do I join the Hare Krishna chant I hear over the intercom before a show. In a small London theatre once, when I was being shown around, I trod on the stomach of a recumbent lady in a yoga trance preparing for her performance, and a radio actor of my acquaintance who retired to a quiet corner and uttered abnormal sounds before arriving at the microphone. I have also worked with excellent actors who gave top performances after a warm-up of strong coffee and a couple of fags.

My first sortie into the alien territory of Northern Ireland was after my father's transfer to Monaghan in 1931. It was also the first time I saw an Orange parade. Strange beings these Orangemen were, sashed and bowler-hatted, stepping it out to fife and drum in the wake of an unsheathed sword. But the Twelfth of July was their day and, without hostility, my family watched them parade. Had we thought about it we would have allowed that Catholics must have appeared odd to Orangemen when we wore Confraternity sashes and sang hymns in the wake of a golden monstrance processed under a golden canopy. But we didn't think about it. We looked on the Orangemen as curiosities in our world of RC normality.

Two Lyric actors of different creeds, both liberal of outlook, walked together on the day following an atrocity. One said, 'When something like this happens, is it your instinct to hope it's the other crowd, not yours, who are responsible?' 'Yes,' was the morose reply, 'it's in the gut.'

While still a boy I crossed the Border at my father's side to attend an international soccer match in Windsor Park. At Goraghwood we said 'Nothing to declare' when Her Majesty's Customs searched for smuggled goods. We marvelled at the *Prepare To Meet Thy God* painted with Armageddon thunder on a Portadown gable. Our journey to Windsor Park was flanked by meeting houses and Gospel halls that warned of imminent hellfire. The RUC wore uniforms of forbidding black. Revolvers hung on hips. School lore knew for certain that the RUC hated Catholics. A classmate's elder brother, in digs in Portadown, reported that a housemaid claimed that Papishes ate babies. 'Rubbish,' my father grunted. Nevertheless, to be on the safe side, I adopted what I believed to be a Protestant look when a constable glanced my way.

The thundering words on that Portadown gable came sharply into focus years later when driving North on a Sunday. I took a wrong turn and stopped in Lurgan to ask directions. The street was deserted but for a small, wrinkled man hobbling on a stick. I lowered the car window. 'Excuse me, I'm looking for the most direct way to Derry.' The man's body was frail but not his voice. Like an Old Testament prophet he boomed, 'Brother, are you saved?'

That took the wind out of my sails. The little man boomed on. He had fought in the trenches in the First World War. He had drunk and hoored and lived an evil life, but now he was saved. Was I saved, Brother? Was I saved?

I assured him that, like himself, I aspired to heaven. Stepping back from the car he wished me well. He had not given me any directions about how to reach Derry but I drove on rather than ask and risk being saved once more. I left him resting on his stick, the sole human on an empty street in Lurgan on a Sunday. That man and I, both Irishmen, lived no more than sixty miles apart, but we were separated as surely by culture and tradition as if a tempestuous ocean rolled between us.

To balance the scales against that chance meeting in Lurgan, let me recall a conversation I had in County Clare with another Irishman. Over a cup of tea I mentioned casually that I had recently been in Belfast for a month. He was incredulous. 'Belfast? Up there?' Had he been to Belfast? I asked, knowing full well what his answer would be. No, he cried, nor ever crossed the Border, nor ever would. His voice rose, 'They should all to go back.'

'Who?' I asked, as if I couldn't guess.

'The Protestants,' he declared, 'to England where they came from.'

I let things rest for a time before asking how long his family had lived in Clare. Ninety years or more, he told me. The Protestants, I said, had lived in the North for three hundred years, Ulster was their birthplace and their home. If I thought this would silence him I was wrong. 'What right had they to come here in the first place?' he demanded, and that concluded our political discussion.

In the early seventies I was invited by Mary O'Malley to direct in the Lyric. The Troubles were at their height. Tension in the city was palpable. It dropped from the clattering helicopters, it seeped from bombed buildings, shattered glass, checkpoints, Saracen trucks, and the guns of soldiers crouched in doorways. It was bomb scares, it was coming face to face in a laneway near the Lyric with an army patrol, guns at the ready, twisting this way and that in the ritual dance of sur-veillance.

Not being of any political significance I could think of no reason why I should be assassinated. But I was cautious, aware that I could be in the wrong place at the wrong time. My daily round was confined within the triangle of the theatre in Ridgeway Street, the rehearsal room in Cromwell Road and Ulsterville Avenue, where I was staying with my friend Joe McPartland and his wife Pauline. In the evenings I worked on a play I was to direct later in the year for Gemini and dis-covered how easy it was to grow accustomed to the sound of distant rifle fire. If it commenced later than usual, I glanced at my watch and wondered what had delayed the guns.

Distant firing heard from a quiet room in a quiet house on a quiet avenue was no more than the unthreatening background sound effects in a political drama, but guns just down the road were a rude reality; the house vibrating – I was astonished by the loudness – lights out, keeping clear of the windows, the half-light from the street eerie on drawn blinds.

My brush with the Troubles was trivial, but it was enough to make me wonder what it was like to live in a nationalist or unionist area hemmed-in by guns. Does a gun breed dreams of glory as a defender of tradition, a fighter for the cause? Does it justify responsibility for the death it might cause? It is easy to theorise, easy to grab the high moral ground. My experience was no more than a diverting dinner table anecdote when I returned south, but working in Belfast I soon learned that in East or West Belfast it was Orange or Green, with no dilution of the colours in between.

The Lyric was established by Mary O'Malley, which, bearing in mind her antipathy towards the political regime that reigned north of the border, was a remarkable achievement. An unwavering enthusiast for the theatre, her adventure commenced in a tiny premises in Derryvolgie Avenue, where she gathered around her a group of dedicated players who performed in a space I imagine to have been the equivalent of the 37 Theatre Club. From Derryvolgie bloomed the Lyric Theatre, to succeed triumphantly in providing international and contemporary local drama for a Belfast audience. Not the least of the theatre's achievements was that throughout the Troubles, but for one night during the Workers' Strike, like the Windmill during the war it never closed, not even on the night a bomb exploded in the alleyway adjoining the theatre.

From Ibsen to Brian Friel, from Bernard Shaw to Graham Reid, from Anton Chekhov to Willie Russell, the list of Lyric productions is impressive. My first engagement was to direct Brian Friel's *The Gentle Island*, a production, it delighted me to learn, that pleased the author. Later I would direct regularly in the theatre; among the plays were Shaw's *Saint Joan*, Willie Russell's *Educating Rita* and Dion Boucicault's *The Colleen Bawn*, in the rehearsal for which a tall young actor caught my eye. But it was not until he made his entrance on the first night, wearing a period costume and commanding the stage, that I recognised in him more than the skills of a talented player. Here was an actor with that extra something, that indefinable ability, to quote Orson Wells, to displace air. He was, of course, Liam Neeson.

The Lyric provided a ready stage for authors who reviewed the contemporary political situation; Brian Friel, Patrick Galvin, for a time writer in residence, John Boyd, Graham Reid, Jennifer Johnston and Gary Mitchell come immediately to mind. Wilson John Hare's *Between Two Shadows* was produced in the seventies, and Gemini, believing it to be a play that ought be seen in the south, decided to stage it. I directed a cast led by Doreen Hepburn, Joe McPartland and Dermot Crowley. We opened in the Cork Opera House, played to poor houses, and did not transfer to Dublin. Interest in the struggle in the North, I sometimes thought, was in inverse proportion to distance from the Border. Too often I heard no more of the Northern struggle than, 'If you cross the Border, keep your head down,' or 'Surely to God there's something else to talk about on the radio than the bloody North.' Indifference is less taxing than understanding.

I regretted what I thought to be small audiences for the quality of work delivered by the Lyric. The theatre suffered from the disadvantage of location – how many from West Belfast supported the Lyric? Conversely, how many from Stranmillis supported the West Belfast

Festival? The Lyric company toured widely in Northern Ireland, and broke new ground by travelling south to take part in the Dublin Theatre Festival, but I detected little enthusiasm to bring performances across the city to West Belfast. One must live in Belfast to appreciate the vast ideological gulf that divides the city; Prods and Taigs, *To Hell with the Pope*, *Brits out* – there's no escape. Even in the third strand of the Northern tangle, the well-groomed avenues, unruffled and aloof, where, the joke ran, they fought with sponges, where apparent tolerance was a by-product of social advantage, I do not doubt that conviction lay as deep as in East or West Belfast. But concern for economic security came first, as well as the maintenance of a firm hand on the tiller of power.

When I returned to the Lyric in the nineties to play in *Lengthening Shadows*, Belfast was a changed city. The buzz of youth was on the streets and in the bars. After dark I walked the city centre with less apprehension than I walk in Dublin, where druggies mug an old lady for her handbag, and another gangland murder is regularly the top item on the national news. I live alone. I lock the front door after dark, and have a cautious look outside before answering a knock. With regret I recall that in Nancy's time the back door of Salmon was always on the latch.

When I returned to the Lyric for *Lengthening Shadows*, Mary O'Malley had retired and others had taken over. It was strange not to feel her presence throughout the building. She had ruled the stage, the auditorium, the offices and even the foyer. Today a bust to mark her contribution to the theatre overlooks the stairs to the auditorium, but too many do not appreciate her achievement in establishing the Lyric from small beginnings, and what the artistic life of Belfast owes to her tenacity and vision.

8

Most days are routine. Not all. On the 21st of May 1999, I was on call for a part in *Ballykissangel*. My pick-up was at 5.30. Nancy was sleeping when I left.

The first day on location is a first day at school. You are not one of the gang. The make-up people are young. 'How'r ya, Harry? Sorry, Barry. Are you from Dublin? Where? Oh yeah.' Now you know who you are. Humility is good for the soul and all that jazz.

Niall Toibin arrived. Saw me in the make-up mirror. 'Ah me ould friend.' My stock rose.

After make-up and costume – I was playing a priest – I was despatched to familiarise myself with the car in which I would arrive at the door of the presbytery. It was the latest model, God knows how many thousand smackers plus, the sort of upmarket vehicle I had never driven, nor ever expected to drive, nor had ever seen a priest drive, nor ever expected to see one drive, not even a flamboyant bishop. But mine not to reason why, mine but to drive the thing, take the money and run. So, under instruction, I swanned around the roads of Wicklow commanding envious looks at the glistening machine and not a little surprise at the clerical collar behind the wheel.

That was the easy bit. When it came to shooting I had to drive into shot at the presbytery door. Things didn't go well. For all the splendour of the mighty motor, even with the driving seat extended to the limit, it did not comfortably accommodate my six feet three. Disembarking was a graceless wriggle from under a steering wheel that pinioned my legs. What was more, the car was automatic, something unfamiliar to me. Try as I might, I arrived in a series of buck-leaps that pleased neither cameraman nor director.

In my final shot I was to be greeted by Niall at the presbytery door. We were standing by for a take when a young woman walked onto the set. Odd, I thought, no one walks onto a set when a camera is about to roll. The young woman handed me a note. It read, 'Nancy in hospital. Ring Philip.'

Nancy in hospital? Nancy, who was never ill? Nancy, who at seventy-one stood on the top step of an A-ladder to pin up a border when helping out at the local festival, scaring the daylights out of those younger and fitter who watched in awe? Nancy, who drove tractors, worked in the fields, played golf and gave not a damn for wind or weather? Nancy, whose rude health was a family joke? An accident, I feared. 'Where's the nearest phone?'

Niall handed me his mobile.

I rang my son Philip. 'Nancy is in Beaumont,' he told me. 'She collapsed this afternoon and was taken there by ambulance. I didn't know where you were. I had to ring around. I got through as quickly as I could.'

'What's wrong?'

'They didn't say.'

The film company – I am ever grateful – got me away as quickly as possible; one take, my day clothes hurried from my caravan, a taxi waiting to drive me to Beaumont.

At the hospital the family had gathered. From Andrew I learned what had happened. In the afternoon Nancy was driving around the farm in a pick-up, fast enough for Andrew, our farming son, to ask her to take it easy. She was impatient to get back to the garden. 'It's my bloody truck,' he protested. Not that she slowed down. Back at Salmon she went to the garden. Some time later she rang Andrew. 'Come to the house.' Her tone was enough. He found her collapsed in a chair beside the phone.

He rang for an ambulance. 'She's unconscious,' he said.

'I'm not,' she said.

In A&E she lay behind screens, on her side as I had often seen her at night when she had gone to bed before me and was half-asleep. She was pale, but no paler than I had seen her many mornings of late when she was silent at breakfast and did not answer when I spoke. Irritating me. Touchiness. Now I understand her silence. We always understand when it is too late.

I whispered, 'We're all here. We've come to bring you home.' I had no doubt we would, if not that evening then the next day. Death did not enter my mind.

In pairs we were allowed to sit with her. Time passed. Time weighed down with growing worry. Time not measured by the clock but by the tremulous heart.

We were requested to leave her bedside. From a distance we did not miss a move of the comings and goings to and from the screens behind which she lay. A doctor explained that she had not had a heart attack. Another that she had not suffered a stroke. They were conducting tests, they said.

It was late night now, the small, bloodless hours. The hospital somnolent. An unreal world. But this was no sensational TV series where ambulances shriek, orderlies career down corridors pushing stretchers, white coats shout, and TV panic rules. This was reality, the lengthening late hours of anxiety and silent watch.

A drunk reeled in. Tried to make conversation. 'He's here every night,' a nurse explained. Then added without rancour, 'God help him.'

A flurry behind the screens. A nurse dashing out. Disappearing. Returning as fleetly. All eyes on the screens. Riveted. Again the nurse leaving and returning as swiftly.

For the first time thoughts of death stirred. Did I pray? I don't remember. Life is no artless tale from a devotional magazine. The drowning man utters no final prayer, he gasps for life and has no other thought. I wanted life for Nancy. I knew no more. Existence shrank to a burning point of fearing for her life and wanting her to live. To be returned to me. To all of us. I did not own her. Never did. She belonged to all of us, gave herself to all of us, and that is why she was so dearly loved.

The doctor returned to tell us she was sleeping and they were moving her to a ward. My heart lifted. I reassured myself that if her condition was serious it was not to a ward they would transfer her but to intensive care. Her bed was in the corner of a ward, the accoutrements of illness surrounding her: tubes, a drip, a monitor spinning out a graph of heartbeats, like stock television without the camera, no senior actress made pale by make-up, no out-of-shot crew whispering life and love and where the party is tonight.

Some in the ward slept, some lay awake. At the door two nurses whispered and kept watch, the prime of their youth in sharp contrast to those who lay in bed, old and ailing, clinging to what was left of life. Nancy would not be one of them. She would sleep, she would wake, we would bring her home.

Two o'clock. Tiredness and strain taking their toll. Nancy sleeping. There seemed no reason for everyone to remain in the hospital, so a watch was arranged; James, our eldest son, and his wife Mary would see out the night, Philip would take over at seven in the morning. I was encouraged to go home but I remained.

In an adjoining room I lay in a reclining chair, but I could not sleep and returned to sit at the foot of Nancy's bed. The monitor above it held my eye, its graph zigzagging across the screen, the only movement in a ward hushed to silence by the lateness of the hour. On and on the graph zigzagged. Across the screen and off, across and off, start again. Seismic measurement. Richter scale. Lie detector. Life and death detector. Was I apprehensive? I do not think so. My thoughts were for the morning to come and for Nancy to have recovered.

In an alarming instant the pattern on the monitor altered; the zigzags were replaced by flat lines that raced across, up, down to the bottom of the screen, up again to centre then off the other side. Repeat. And again. And again before the regular pattern returned.

A nurse turned the screen her way for better viewing. If anything was seriously wrong, I assured myself, the nurse would have detected it and taken action.

The adrenaline that had sustained me for twenty-four hours began to fail. At four o'clock James said I must have rest. He would drive me home. I studied the monitor. The pattern was regular. Nancy was sleeping normally. It was safe to go. At seven Philip would take over. He would ring and tell me how she was.

I was home about half-four. In bed I fell asleep at once.

From a blank void of exhaustion Sinead, Andrew's wife, who lives nearby and holds a key, was in my bedroom shaking me awake. Nancy had suffered cardiac arrest. Cardiac arrest? The term did not immediately register as 'heart attack'. New term, old man.

Sinead drove fast – if Eddie Jordan ever needs a driver – eyes fixed ahead on the unwinding road. Cardiac arrest – the hospital would deal with it . . .

In the hospital Sinead led me through darkened hallways. At the end of a dim corridor I distinguished Philip and knew at once why he was waiting. Without preamble, he said, quietly, 'She's dead.'

I remember saying, 'I wasn't here.'

Shock is a Perspex screen. One can see through but is not part of outside reality. Philip took my hand, my child took my hand and I was grateful, and led me to the ward. The family was at her bedside. Lost for words.

Death is a glacier, momentous, drifting away, away.

A chaplain came, offering to say prayers. I welcomed him. Do some reject him? Because they do not believe? Because the habit of praying was never learned or is forgotten? Because, to them, a chaplain represents a God without pity?

We bowed our heads and listened, seeking comfort in our anguish.

It was explained that there must be a postmortem and that it would be Monday before we could remove Nancy from the hospital, before we could bring her home. For home she must come. To Salmon. Her home. She must return so that family and neighbours could bid her a fitting farewell. No funeral parlour for her, with its mawkish music and air of convenient disposal.

Sunday was unreal. Had Nancy lain in Salmon it would have been easier, she would have been with her family, her family with her, but in our minds it was all too easy to imagine her in the chill anonymity of a hospital morgue.

On Monday we brought her home. When the hearse pulled to the front of the house Father Michael was waiting. Rain began to fall. Someone whispered, 'It's weeping for Nancy.' The sentiment was kindly meant but to me the rain was rain and no more than rain. Nature does not weep. It does not smile. It does not vent joy or spleen upon mankind. It turns the wheel of time while some are born and some must die, as Nancy died.

Prayers were said before the coffin was carried to the trestles waiting in the dining room. It did not fit easily through the kitchen door and had to be tilted. I could not bear to think of her disturbed but before I could intervene it was through and we waited outside until she was readied by the undertaker for her wake.

Friends and neighbours crowded the house. Tales were told of her. Grandchildren she greatly loved kissed her goodbye, the littlest held aloft to look on her. Two farming men, good neighbours, wearing their Sunday best, knew the older ways better than most and used the sprig of palm to sprinkle the Sign of the Cross on her with Holy Water, then drew their beads to say a decade of the Rosary.

Late in the evening Father Michael returned to say night prayers. Younger people did not understand, but when I called on them to come and pray for Nancy, they crowded to where she lay and listened to the words spoken by the priest, words of majesty and wisdom that did not blur but clarified, and, to those who believe, assuaged the finality of death. When all had left, I sat a while alone with her, still finding it hard to believe that she was dead.

Next evening came another parting, for there are many partings at a time of death. The coffin must be sealed before her removal to the church. We kissed her forehead, I the last. My privilege. Then, following the hearse, her family accompanied her on her last journey down Salmon lane. She had lived her life in Salmon, had been a schoolgirl there, had farmed the land, had married from Salmon, had raised her family there. Nancy was Salmon. Salmon was Nancy. In my lifetime, and in the lifetime of her children, so it will always be.

For more than an hour in the church my hand was pressed. In grief we need our hands to be pressed, to accept the murmured 'Sorry for your trouble,' 'A terrible shock,' 'My sympathies,' words that link the generations in grief, that remind us that the world spins once each day, shedding sorrow with its spume, that remind us we are not alone in grief, that brace us for the loneliness that lies ahead.

Next day, at Mass, the church choir sang, and Geraldine O'Grady played for Nancy, who had been her friend. Anne, our eldest child, paid a tribute on behalf of our children, and I – because our love had prospered through thirty-eight years, calmer and more firm in the later years, lifting my heart each time I turned into Salmon lane to see Salmon house before me and know she would be waiting – spoke of her with words of loss and words of humour, as is the way we seek to deal with death.

Gravity attends a funeral, the black of mourning, the black of clergy, the family first behind the hearse, the measured pace of the procession, window blinds drawn, shop blinds drawn, hats raised, life's bustle slowed for a respectful moment in witness of a life's ending. At the graveside a little grandchild stretched out his arms and I held him while prayers were said and the coffin lowered. Will a memory remain with him of the burial of his grandmother? A graven snapshot of the deep pit and lowering coffin? I hope so. I am greedy that all should remember her.

Her grave was deeper than any I had ever stood beside. Deep enough to shrink her coffin in its depth. Another parting. The final one.

In time shock fades, but neither loss nor loneliness do.

From a window I look over the land of Salmon and find it hard to grasp that she is gone. I do not rail at God, or Fate, or what it was that took her off, but nothing will ever be the same.

Places recall the past. As do fleeting images. From nowhere the past arises to haunt with an intensity that brings tears. Between Monasterevin and Kildare a straight section of road traverses low-lying, rushy land. On the way home from our honeymoon I was driving when we passed that way. It was raining, a fine misty rain that veiled the countryside. A great black car swept by, flooding us with spray. That is all, nothing dramatic, but when I pass that way the vision returns and I am driving into a new life with a young woman at my side who will bring to my future all that is best and most enduring.

Since Nancy's death I have lived alone. For the first few years in Salmon, then at the end of Salmon lane, in a house built by my youngest son, Andrew, who runs the farm. From the sun room I look towards the old house and observe the Hill Field as it marks the passing of the seasons from tillage to greening to the gold of a flourishing crop, a view at its most arresting when the sun is low in the west and autumn shadows lengthen into twilight.

The curious and the concerned ask if I still drive. If I did not, I assure them, I would be isolated, dependent on family, neighbours and the ministrations of home help for the rudiments of existence. I walk with the aid of a stick. I am a master of the microwave. I have a laugh with the girls at the cash desks in the supermarket. On Sundays I have lunch in the local hotel where I have a word for everyone. I daresay I have become a bit of a local character. I shall fight for my independence until the bitter end. Lord defend me from the nursing home and the jabbering television, to sit propped in an invalid chair between the gaga lady and the snoring denizen of man's seventh age.

Beyond Balbriggan Harbour a cliff runs north along the coast. In youth I walked that way with friends, skirting the ruins of a stone cottage that stood near the cliff edge. With the passing years the tide clawed at the cliff beneath. First fell the seaward wall, then the gables, finally the wall on the landward side. No trace of the cottage now remains. Even the fallen walls have been subsumed into the rocky foreshore. Erosion took the old house stone by stone, as the years take life. So what? Make the best of what is left; the alternative is extreme.

Thus endeth the first lesson.

For the last few years I have not undertaken to direct plays – there is a particular energy required for directing that I have lost – not that any management has come banging on my door demanding my services. In the mirror I nod 'Hello' to the Day Before Yesterday's Man. So be it. It was good while it lasted.

When Patricia Hayes was complimented on continuing to perform into her late years, she declared that 'The opposition is dying off.' In the declining years there are always bits and pieces for the old; the grandparent who is boringly benign, an expiring ancient in a hospital bed, a senile grandfather in a rocking chair (I have one) the cause of marital strife because the wife will not agree to putting him in a home, even a horror film ancient in a nightshirt fleeing from the risen dead. I have been luckier than that. On the walls of my small office are photographs to commemorate rewarding parts that came my way in my final years on the stage.

It was never my habit to collect programmes or compile a scrapbook to document my comet-like sweep across the theatrical firmament of the twentieth century. Jumbled in a drawer are bits and pieces cut at random from newspapers, among them a photograph of Lisa Dwan and myself in costume for a children's series called *Mystic Knights of Tir na nOg*. I played Cathbad, a benevolent druid and first minister to the king. Like all the best druids, I was garbed in flowing robes, wore a long beard and a wig that reached below my shoulders. The series was financed from America. The first reports to reach us were that it was running well in the States, so well that McDonald's decided to make dolls of the leading characters for distribution with their products. But not of me. Only dolls of the youthful warriors who battled the evil forces of Queen Maebh would apparently encourage young America to consume more Big Macs. I would like to have been a doll, to stand proudly on the mantelpiece flanked by Mozart and Tutankhamen. The series lasted a year and was cancelled without warning, causing my doll-less career to end and life return to normal.

If I failed to become a doll, I did become a poster. A framed copy hangs on my office wall, recalling a successful reading for the part of the Old Man in *Twelve Angry Men*, staged in Andrew's Lane. The engagement renewed a friendship with Patricia Moylan and Breda Cashe, theatre managers with keen eyes for a winner, and with director Terry Byrne, all of whom I met regularly when I was adjudicating on the amateur drama circuit.

The play enjoyed a long run in Andrew's Lane, was revived, played in both the Olympia and the Gaiety, and did a national tour. In the Cork Opera House, to my astonishment, I became a poster. The theatre manager, Gerry Barnes, was looking through the production photographs when one of them, a group including myself, caught his eye, and he decided to isolate me and use my image on the show card. The show card was used for the remainder of the run, and when we played in the Olympia a large version hung outside the theatre. Every evening on my way backstage I passed a gathering of customers waiting for the box office to open, and it would be gratifying to record that I was mobbed for autographs. But not a single member of the public thrust an autograph book, or even a scruffy envelope, under my nose. Fame at last!

A striking photograph on my wall is that of ten people enjoying a celebratory meal at a long table. The play is *Festen*, staged in the Gate in 2006. I had a long association with the Gate. It was a regular venue for Nora Lever and myself in the days of 37, and even earlier, in drama student days, I paid my shilling for a seat in the back row for performances by Longford Productions or Edwards/Mac Liammóir of a range of plays from Farquhar to Congreve, from Chekhov to Wilde. Later, when I sat closer to the stage, the result of ready money or a complimentary seat, I saw the work of T. S. Eliot and Christopher Fry, both of whose plays are now ignored, as are the plays of Christine Longford, most memorably *Yahoo*, her play on Jonathan Swift. My late engagements in the Gate were under the management of Michael Colgan, whose tenure in the Gate brought back to the theatre a lustre not seen since the best days of Edwards and Mac Liammóir.

My agents, First Call, arranged for me to do an interview for the part of Grandfather in *Festen*, to be directed by Selina Cartmell, a bright talent working in the Irish theatre. A photograph on the wall proves that I got the part. The action of the play revolves around the celebration of the father's sixtieth birthday. In a speech delivered by his son, it is disclosed that he raped his children, a theme that would not have reached the stage in the days of Censorship Boards and Leagues of Decency. But this was 2006. A torrent of scandal concerning clerical paedophilia was rocking the Catholic Church and undermining its influence. Change is not achieved without a price, and if I regret the prevalence of drugs, the regularity of murders, and gangland shootings in the streets, I welcome the new freedom, a freedom of the mind, an escape from the iron-fisted dominance of Church and State that outlawed independent thinking in the Ireland of my youth.

I have no photograph to celebrate at last making it to the stage of the Abbey, in 1997. By then the Abbey was far different from the Abbey of my early years; the idea of a permanent company had been abandoned and fluency in Irish was no longer essential to appearing in the National Theatre. Audiences, freed from the insularity of the early and middle parts of the twentieth century, had been guided by such talented artistic directors as Tomás Mac Anna and Joe Dowling into a policy that not only reflected contemporary Ireland but was ready to explore ideas from beyond our national boundaries.

An invitation from Conall Morrison offered me a part in his adaptation of Patrick Kavanagh's *Tarry Flynn*. Connell is an imaginative director with more than a touch of adventure in his work. I played Father Daly, who is harried in a comic scene by a barking dog mimed by an actor on all fours snapping at my heels. A lady who had known the real Father Daly was displeased with my performance. The real Father Daly, she claimed, was a cultured man, not the uncouth figure I presented. I explained that I was playing Father Daly as Kavanagh presented him, not the genuine one, but she remained stone-faced and disapproving both of me and of Patrick Kavanagh.

I have no photograph from *Tarry Flynn* to decorate my wall, but on my windowsill stand two photographs from *The Dandy Dolls*, also directed by Conall, in the Peacock in 2004. Dressed in grey and topped by a grey tall hat, I played the Grey Man in a production of great energy and clouds of smoke. After detailed rehearsals and a six-week run, I am not certain that I fully understood Fitzmaurice's fantasy. Which raises a question I have long pondered; if an actor understands the character he portrays, is it essential for him to grasp every nuance of the play? Or can he leave the overall interpretation in the hands of the director and concentrate solely on his part? (Do I speak heresy? Am I to sizzle in the fires on some theatrical stake?) Bernard Shaw had a view on such matters, or perhaps a put-down of mere actors, when he put words in the mouth of Nell Gwynn in *In Good King Charles's Golden Days*: asked to reveal the plot of the play in which she was appearing, Nell answered with some surprise, 'How would I know? I only know my lines.'

My last time under the roof of the National Theatre was when I played in *The Burial at Thebes*, Seamus Heaney's adaptation of *Antigone*. Patrick Mason directed with incisive subtlety and the action of the translation moved effortlessly. The dialogue was easy to deliver, so different from translations of classic texts that labour under the literal exactness of meticulous academics with no gift for theatrics.

Few distinguished men or women carry their honours, their talent and their achievements with such unaffected ease as Seamus Heaney. That he was pleased with the production gave everyone, cast and director, a feeling of genuine achievement. I am pleased to have a photograph and poster of *The Burial at Thebes* on my wall. It may have been my last performance on stage; if so, I could finish off with nothing better.

Dublin is fortunate in the standard of its two main theatres, the Abbey and the Gate. Add the Druid in Galway, led by Garry Hynes, and the theatre in Ireland is in the healthiest state I've known since I became an actor in the 1940s.

In the early days of Druid, I saw the young company perform at a Listowel Writers' Week, and remarked to a professional friend that there was a big future ahead of the group. An eyebrow was raised, and, later, I was subjected to a sly dig about my 'little amateur friends from Galway.'

'Give them ten years,' I said. We did not have to wait so long.

In Waterford is Red Kettle. I directed for the company in that interesting period when the group, guided by Jim Nolan and T. V. Honan, was progressing from the amateur world to the professional. Jim Nolan is a gifted writer. Before we met, before the days of Red Kettle, I was given a script to read by Michael Scott when he was directing the Dublin Theatre Festival. The author's name was missing but the quality of the writing reminded me of *The Gods Are Angry, Miss Kerr*, an early play by Jim that I had read. Was the author a chap from Waterford, I wondered? Yes, Michael told me. The play he had given me to read was *The Boathouse*, and it was produced in the 1986 Dublin Theatre Festival with Mary McEvoy in the cast. A spectacular set was designed by Barbara Bradshaw. It stood on stilts surrounded by water, which caused the production manager to question the feasibility of setting up such a structure on the floor of the SFX theatre, where the play would be produced. Michael Scott intervened and told the production people to get on with it, which they did in style, erecting the set on a base of plastic filled with water. Of such stuff are festivals directors made.

A time comes when facts must be faced. That I might not be fit enough to play in the theatre for much longer was a thought that flickered before being cursorily dismissed. But time plods on with reminders of Una's line in *The Countess Cathleen*, 'The years like great black oxen tread the world and I am broken by their passing feet.'

The passing feet caught up with me in the Gate during rehearsals for *The Old Curiosity Shop*, in which I had been engaged to play Grandfather. All went well for the first week of rehearsal, then things changed and I was dragging myself daily to and from the theatre. I warned Alan Stanford, who was directing, that perhaps he had better start thinking about a replacement. I consulted a doctor. Would I be fit enough to carry on? That, she answered wisely, I would know without her having to tell me. Her answer left me with little choice; if I was forced to withdraw late in rehearsal, the company would be faced with finding a replacement at the last minute; if I said nothing and dropped out suddenly during the run, the replacement problem would be even more acute.

I had a word with Alan and continued to rehearse until a replacement was found. At my request, nothing was said to the company until I had left the theatre on my last day. I drove home at a steady pace, trying to make a normal day out of an abnormal one.

I remembered an old actor from my time in London. He had one line, just one, in a television drama about the fall of Charles Stewart Parnell, in which I played Tim Healy to Patrick McGoohan's Parnell. When the famous exchange arrived – Parnell's 'I am the master of this party,' and Healy's infamous reply, 'And who is its mistress?' – the old actor's business was to rise between us with a cry of, 'Gentlemen, Gentlemen, please.' Came the lines, came the cue. The old actor struggled to his feet, trembled, stuttered, stammered. No line emerged.

This was live television. The director could not shout *Cut!* and re-run the scene. The cameras churned on and the pause extended until McGoohan picked things up and we carried on.

After the transmission the director was in a fury. 'I was asked to find something for that man because he was out of work for some time and hard-up. Never again will I allow sentiment to come before a show.'

At the time I had little sympathy for the old actor who had failed. Now it was my turn, and it was no consolation that I had had a run of over sixty years on the stage, nor that if I had hung on for a few more days I could have done the play. Alan and the management were sympathetic, but I know the ways of the theatre, I know the rules, and, like the failed actor in the television drama, I did not expect to be asked back.

Have I retired? Officially? Have I raised the white flag? Not yet. I have recently played small parts in films.

Down the road lives a friend, Bunny. In the morning we have conversations across a hedge when he is walking his greyhounds on the road and I am feeding the birds in the front garden. He noted that a taxi had come to collect me for an early morning call. 'Are you not retired yet?'

'Should I be?'

'You're well past retiring age.'

In my spry, green years, to 'retire' meant to move into a hoary world of growing cabbage in the back garden, whist-drives, and St Vincent de Paul (middle class) or to have squatter's rights on a seat in the snug (working class) or to occupy an armchair by the fire ('Get the dog off Granda's chair or there'll be war!') or to ramble on about times long-gone and forgotten by all but other boring old men of any class whose short-term memory is shot to pieces and whose long-term memory dwells in a never-never land of the past.

With the passing years my retiring age extended. In my youth I considered sixty a proper age at which to go. As sixty approached, I pushed it up to seventy. Then seventy-five. Then eighty. Now I might as well shop 'til I drop.

The course of my life was not determined by planning. In common with many an actor I moved from one engagement to the next like one crossing a river by irregular stepping-stones. When I was dark of hair and fair of countenance, I gave but a passing thought to retiring, but now, this man Bunny – a friend, mark you – had brought up the subject. He had retired so long before that it required an effort to remember him behind the counter of his shop. Now he indulges his hobbies to the full; golf and greyhounds, breeding them, walking them, racing them. Friendly creatures, greyhounds. They win my sympathy. Ever ready for a friendly pat, one wonders what happens to them when they can no longer make fast times on the track.

'Why should I retire?' I asked, quoting the old theatre joke that 'old actor's don't retire; people stop giving them work.' As long as work is on offer, as long as the limbs hold and lines can be memorised, an actor is in business. Not that he any longer expects to play the faithful husband or the passionate lover, but there may be a few lines as a sage, or a famine victim, or a dying hospital patient. I died in *The Clinic*, in *Killinascully*, and in a couple of short films. In *Jack Taylor* I was knocked down in the street. A lady of my acquaintance wondered when I was going to live, and was not amused when I told her I was rehearsing for the real thing. Not that I want my make-up box on my coffin when the time comes. God forbid.

Why do actors bother to go on acting beyond the time when most people have put their feet up? Because acting is their game. Skill? Craft? Art? The ability to act is not a unique gift handed down by the Gods. All over the world there are actors whose talent ranges from the brilliant to the run-of-the-mill, which can be said of any occupation or profession. The owner of the corner shop is in the same game as Sir Anthony O'Reilly; he just hasn't been as successful.

If the Gods put a thumb-mark on the forehead of the fortunate one, then he or she is blessed. Stardom lies ahead. I was not fated to have a thumb-mark on my forehead, except the priest's thumb-mark on Ash Wednesday. I enjoyed my life in the theatre. I aimed to make a living as a capable professional and can claim to have managed that. No doubt, had stardom come along I would have accepted with open arms the risks of drink, drugs and unprotected sex, but, early on, I had enough cop not to pine hopelessly for the unattainable. Well, that's my story, and I'm sticking to it.

Acknowledgements

My thanks to Anne Cassin for her unfailing assistance when this book was in preparation for publication.

To Jonathan Williams, who suffered a blizzard of misspellings on his way to finding a publisher, my most sincere thanks.

A special thanks to Pauline O'Hare for her assistance and eagle eye as a proofreader and to Art O'Hare for his patience with a computer illiterate.

Thanks to Eugene McCabe, who was the first to read the finished manuscript; his good opinion encouraged me to seek a publisher.

My gratitude also to Christy Byrne for his photographic skills. Thanks are due also to the staff at Liberties Press, especially Seán O'Keeffe, Dan Bolger and Caroline Lambe.

Finally, my deepest thanks to all the members of my family, whose support made the writing of this memoir possible.

Index